Juniper Hall

Juniper Hall

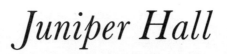

An English Refuge from the
French Revolution

Linda Kelly

WEIDENFELD AND NICOLSON
LONDON

First published in 1991 by
George Weidenfeld & Nicolson Ltd
91 Clapham High Street, London SW4 7TA

British Library Cataloguing in Publication Data
applied for

ISBN 0 297 81078 2

Typeset at The Spartan Press Ltd,
Lymington, Hants

Printed in Great Britain by
Butler & Tanner Ltd,
Frome and London

Contents

Illustrations

Acknowledgements

I would like to thank the librarian of the Henry W. and Albert A. Berg Collection at the New York Public Library, and Astor, Lenox and Tilden Foundations for permission to quote from the correspondence of Susanna Elizabeth Burney Phillips, 1792 and 1793; the Trustees of the British Museum for permission to quote from the Barrett Collection of Burney papers amongst the Egerton manuscripts; and the Oxford University Press for permission to quote from the *Journals and Letters of Fanny Burney*, edited by Joyce Hemlow and others. I am also most grateful for help and advice from John Bebbington, Director of the Field Studies Council at Juniper Hall, Mr and Mrs Frank Chapman of Norbury Park, Adrian Berry, Christine Sutherland, Allegra Huston, and last but not least my husband Laurence Kelly.

To Rosanna, Rachel and Nicky

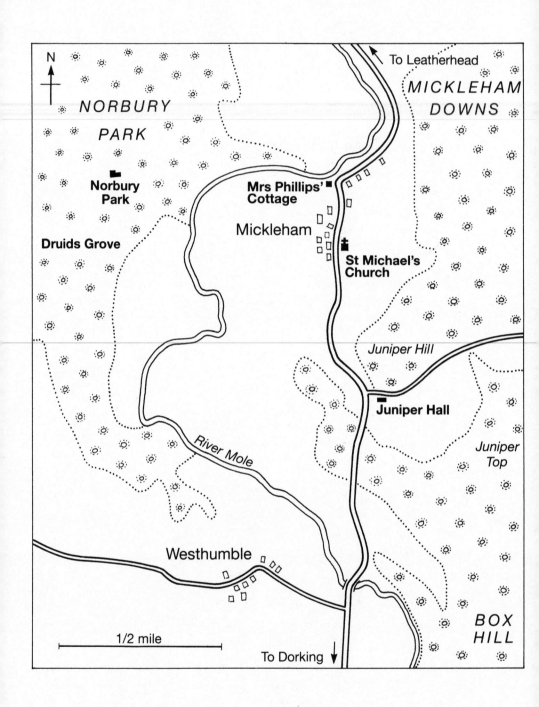

N

NORBURY
PARK

Norbury
Park

Druids Grove

Mrs Phillips'
Cottage

Mickleham

St Michael's
Church

To Leatherhead

MICKLEHAM
DOWNS

Juniper Hill

Juniper Hall

Juniper
Top

River Mole

Westhumble

BOX
HILL

1/2 mile

To Dorking

Preface

Less than twenty miles from London, in one of the loveliest parts of Surrey, the Mickleham valley winds through the wooded chalk hills of the downs near Dorking. At the foot of one such wooded hill, just outside the village of Mickleham, stands Juniper Hall, a substantial eighteenth-century house, set back a little from the road and framed by tall, wide-spreading cedar trees. The house now belongs to the National Trust, on lease to the Field Studies Council as a base for expeditions in the country round about. But a plaque on the gateway, placed there by the Surrey County Council, bears testimony to an earlier, dramatic moment in its history.

'This house,' it reads, 'gave shelter in 1792 to a group of progressive French aristocrats who had fled to England to escape the worst excesses of the French Revolution. The group included the Princesse d'Hénin and Comtesse de la Châtre, Madame de Staël, Jaucourt, Louis de Narbonne, Lally Tollendal, Alexandre d'Arblay and Talleyrand. It was here that Fanny Burney, the novelist, as a visitor to her sister Susanna Phillips of Mickleham, met Alexandre d'Arblay to whom she was subsequently married at Mickleham church.'

It is almost two hundred years since these illustrious visitors, plunged into exile from the heights of fame and power, first took up residence at Juniper Hall. Across the Channel their country was convulsed by war and revolution. Away from the theatre of events, yet passionately concerned in them, they watched and waited for every scrap of news from France. The contrast between the scenes they had left behind and the quiet Surrey countryside was scarcely less great than the contrast of manners and outlook they brought with them. The brilliance of their conversation, their alarmingly progressive views, the irregularity of their amours, sent a frisson through local society. Fanny Burney and her sister were both captivated and appalled. 'Prim little creatures,' wrote Duff Cooper in his life of Talleyrand, 'they had wandered out of the sedate drawing rooms of *Sense and Sensibility* and were in danger of losing themselves in the elegantly disordered alcoves of *Les Liaisons Dangereuses*.'

As Fanny Burney pursued her middle-aged idyll with General d'Arblay, Madame de Staël was at the height of her passion for Louis, Comte de Narbonne, perhaps the greatest of her many loves. She would look back on their time together at Juniper Hall as 'four months of happiness snatched from the shipwreck of my life'. Her letters to Narbonne, fascinating in their depiction of a tumultuous era and emotions equally so, were entrusted to d'Arblay when Narbonne left England on the dangerous journey across Europe to rejoin her. '*Lettres brûlantes à brûler* – a fine moral lesson too,' wrote Fanny Burney primly when she came to arrange her husband's papers.

These letters, considered unsuitable for publication by Fanny Burney's niece Charlotte Barrett when she came to edit her aunt's papers in 1840 – 'beautiful – just like Corinna – *mais* not possible to print' – were relegated to a tin trunk with a section of the Burney archive. They lay there unnoticed till the 1930s when an American collector, Owen D. Young, bought the tin trunk and its contents from a great-great-niece of Fanny Burney, Anna Julia Wauchope. It was his librarian, Sarah A. Dickson, who, in cataloguing the archive, identified the letters, none of them signed and most unaddressed as well. When the papers were sold in their turn to the A. and W. Berg Collection in the New York Public Library, they became accessible to the public and the first edition of the letters was published in France in 1960.

Thanks to these letters, together with Fanny Burney's journals and letters in volumes ii and iii of Joyce Hemlow and her colleagues' magisterial edition, published in 1972 and 1973, and those of her sister

Mrs Phillips (many of them still unpublished), it is possible to build up a far fuller picture of this fascinating interlude than has been possible before. 'This Mickleham episode,' remarked the *Encyclopaedia Britannica* in the entry on Madame de Staël in the famous eleventh edition, 'has never been altogether satisfactorily accounted for.' Today one can at least attempt to do so.

Both Fanny Burney and her sister had a gift for recording conversations, a feat of memory carefully cultivated, which makes it possible to listen, as it were, to the very words of her French friends: Talleyrand joking with Madame de Staël, Narbonne discussing Fanny's marriage with Mrs Phillips. To translate them is to lose something of their charm; where only a few phrases are in question I have left them as they are but in the interests of intelligibility I have translated longer passages. I have of course left the spelling and punctuation of letters in English as they were written.

Eighteenth-century French manners were formal; even in her letters to her lover Narbonne Madame de Staël preserved the formal *'vous'* in all but a few paragraphs. Fanny Burney and Mrs Phillips, as sisters, used each other's Christian names, but Madame de Staël was referred to as such by her friends and I have kept this usage here. (It is currently fashionable to refer to Fanny Burney as Frances Burney, on the grounds that the use of the diminutive, with its somewhat childish connotations, impedes serious judgement of her work. However, since it is her personal life with which I am concerned, I have retained the name by which she was known to her family and friends.)

A final point is one of spelling. William Lock of Norbury Park, the benevolent patron of the French refugees, was said to be related to the great philosopher Locke but his name was spelt without a final 'e' by his contemporaries. It was only at the beginning of the nineteenth century that his son William added the 'e' of the present spelling to his name and it is thus that the Lockes are referred to in the later chapters of the Duchess of Sermoneta's delightful record of the family, *The Locks of Norbury*.

Chapter 1

On 14 July 1792, Louis XVI, with his wife and children, attended the celebrations for the third anniversary of the fall of the Bastille. A huge crowd had gathered in the Champ de Mars but there was nothing festive about its mood. France was at war, its frontiers threatened by the armies of Austria and Prussia. A state of national emergency, *la patrie en danger*, had been declared.

Madame de Staël, wife of the Swedish ambassador and daughter of the former Finance Minister, Jacques Necker, watched the processions from a stand close to the royal family. The Queen's eyes, she wrote, recalling the scene, were blinded by tears; the expression on her face was something she would never forget. Amidst the shouts of the crowd for Pétion, the Jacobin mayor of Paris, the few faint voices that cried *'Vive le roi!'* had the sound of a last farewell. When the time came for the King to make his way to the altar at the far end of the Champ de Mars at which he was to renew his oath of loyalty to the Constitution, she followed his powdered head in the distance amongst the dark unpowdered heads that crowded round him. As he climbed up the steps to the altar he already seemed to her as if he were a sacrificial victim going willingly to his death. He would not appear before the crowd again till the day of his execution.

Less than four weeks later, on the night of 9–10 August, the church bells sounded from all over Paris calling the town to arms. The manifesto of the Duke of Brunswick, commander of the Austro-Prussian forces, threatening Paris with destruction if the King's authority were not restored, had been the provocation for a general uprising. That evening the Paris Commune had been disbanded and an insurrectionary Commune had taken its place. The order had gone out to march on the Tuileries.

All night the monotonous tolling of the bells continued. At seven in the morning the ominous sound of cannon fire announced that the attack on the Tuileries had begun. Madame de Staël, with a few friends, stood at the window of the Swedish embassy in the rue du Bac, uncertain and fearful of what the day would bring, uncertain even if they would survive it. From time to time a message would come from the little group of friends, among them her lover, Comte Louis de Narbonne, who had constituted themselves into an unofficial patrol, keeping guard outside the palace. Like Madame de Staël they had been dedicated to the idea of the constitutional monarchy, whose death knell was now sounding, and most had played a leading part in the earlier stages of the Revolution. Their liberal views having earned them the distrust of the royal family and the antagonism of the courtiers surrounding them, all their offers of help in defending the Tuileries had been rejected. Unable to enter the palace yet ready to die for the King, they wandered round its outskirts, exposing themselves to massacre, as Madame de Staël expressed it, in order to console themselves for not being able to fight.

The events of 10 August, the storming of the Tuileries, the massacre of the Swiss guards, the King's surrender to the National Assembly, took their momentous course. As the day wore on and the fighting inside and around the palace continued, Madame de Staël waited vainly for news of her friends. When a report came through that they had all been seized and massacred she could bear it no longer and, ordering her coach, set out towards the Tuileries in the hopes of rescuing any that survived. On reaching the pont Royal, her coach was stopped by a crowd of men whose silent but expressive gestures made it clear that the killing was still going on across the river. After two hours of fruitless efforts to find out what was happening on the other side she at last got word that all the friends in whom she was most interested were alive, but that most had gone into hiding for fear of arrest.

That evening she set out on foot to find them in the various obscure houses where they had taken refuge, passing doorways where armed men, worn out by the day's slaughter, lay sprawled in drunken stupor. The arrival of a patrol designed to keep order, she wrote, was a signal for all honest people to flee; keeping order, in this context, was no more than an excuse for further bloodshed.

Devoted and loyal as she was to all her friends, Madame de Staël's chief concern as she made her way through the dark streets was for the safety of her lover, Louis de Narbonne. As a former Minister of War and a leader of the liberal or constitutional party, he was hated by the Jacobins. Even before 10 August, when it was suspected he had returned to Paris – he had arrived there three days earlier – his life had been at risk. Had he appeared in public he would almost certainly have been arrested.

Louis, Comte de Narbonne Lara, had been the lover of Madame de Staël for three years. He was a *grand seigneur*, handsome, witty and dissipated, with an atmosphere of romantic mystery surrounding his birth. It was rumoured, and was probably true, that he was a natural son of Louis XV. Contemporary gossip took things further by suggesting that his mother was Louis XV's own daughter, Madame Adelaide, and that the Comtesse de Narbonne had acknowledged him as her son in order to conceal the incestuous truth. This further suggestion was unlikely, but the idea that he was of royal birth was given substance by his Bourbon profile and by his favoured upbringing at Court where Madame Adelaide was his godmother and Louis XVI, four years his senior, his godfather and playmate.

On reaching man's estate Narbonne had run through one fortune and married another in the shape of an heiress, Marie Adelaide de Colothon, from whom he later separated. After numerous liaisons he had fallen under the spell of the young Madame de Staël, recently married to the Swedish ambassador, a good-looking but uninspiring husband whom she already regarded more as a convenience than an equal. Madame de Staël was never a beauty. Her figure was stocky, her complexion poor, her features strongly marked and almost masculine. But her magnificent dark eyes were alight with intelligence and wit and in an age of brilliant conversationalists she was considered the most fascinating talker of the day. 'If I were Queen,' said a contemporary, 'I would command her to talk to me always.'

A study of Rousseau published four years earlier, when she was twenty-two, had established her reputation in the world of letters. Her salon at the Swedish embassy was a meeting place for the leading political and intellectual figures of the day. With the outset of the Revolution it had become a centre for those liberal aristocrats, among them Narbonne, who sought a moderate answer to the country's problems, combining reform with a constitutional monarchy along British lines. Her position as the daughter of the Swiss banker Necker, under whose aegis the States General had been called, and the attraction of his enormous fortune, gave her a uniquely powerful base. She delighted in political intrigue and it was largely thanks to her influence that Narbonne had been appointed Minister of War in 1791, a position he had held till his dismissal in April 1792, frustrated by Jacobins and royalists alike in his attempts to put the nation on a sound military footing. Since then he had served in the army under Lafayette till the worsening political situation had brought him back to Paris in the hopes that even at this late stage something might be done to save the King. The tide of events had run too fast for him. 10 August had seen the ruin of his hopes. The King's doom seemed more and more certain; he himself was on the run.

Baron de Staël had been recalled from Paris but his position as Swedish ambassador gave the embassy a reasonable chance of immunity from the searches for arms and political suspects which were instituted after 10 August. It was here, when all other hiding places had proved too dangerous, that Narbonne sought refuge late one evening. 'He was pale as death though still elegantly dressed,' recalled the embassy chaplain Pastor Gambs who remembered him from earlier meetings as a 'stiff and haughty cavalier'. Now, fearing an immediate search, he spent the night concealed beneath the hangings of the altar in the embassy chapel, emerging next morning, noted Pastor Gambs, in a considerably less brilliant state than he had been the night before.

4

Gambs had not been altogether displeased to see the former Minister of War at a disadvantage, but it was thanks to his help that Madame de Staël was able to arrange for Narbonne's escape. Having made discreet enquiries amongst the German-speaking community, he produced a young Hanoverian doctor, Erich Justus Bollman, who announced himself ready to undertake the enterprise. Bollman, an idealist drawn to Paris by the Revolution, was deeply impressed by Narbonne's calm and courage and by the tearful pleas of Madame de Staël, completely self-forgetful in her anxiety for her lover. The fact that she was six months' pregnant – she was expecting a baby by Narbonne – only heightened the drama of the situation in his eyes.

'A crowd of motives which fortunately did not include the beauty of Madame de Staël – for she was ugly – ran through my mind,' he wrote. 'A woman about to give birth, lamenting the fate of her lover, made an immediate appeal to my imagination. Her tears, a man in danger of his life, the idea of reaching England and bettering my position – all these, against which I could only balance the obvious danger to myself, influenced me simultaneously, transforming a possibility into a firm resolution.'

It was not a moment too soon to think of Narbonne's escape. A few days later a servant reported that warrants against him had been posted at the corner of the rue du Bac and the street was soon after closed by soldiers and a house-to-house search carried out. Narbonne and another fugitive were hidden in an upstairs room, unknown to the embassy servants, but they were bound to be discovered if a thorough search were made. Madame de Staël summoned up all her courage to confront the soldiers. By dint of alternate threats and cajoling she managed to persuade them that they would be breaching international law in entering the embassy of a foreign power and that Sweden, if provoked, would launch an immediate attack on France. 'In this way,' she wrote, 'I was able to lead them back to the door and I thanked God for the extraordinary strength He had given me at that moment.'

The respite could only be temporary. Madame de Staël's relationship with Narbonne was well known; sooner or later more determined searchers would return. The resourceful Bollman, however, had managed to obtain the passport of a Hanoverian friend which, being issued by the British embassy (Hanover was still attached to the British crown), would enable Narbonne to travel as an Englishman. Disguised and in company with Bollman he succeeded in passing the various guard posts on the way to Boulogne without being discovered. 'The word English, the carefree way we showed our passports, and our boldness threw dust in their eyes,' wrote Bollman. 'We talked of the terrifying events in Paris, and the way the English saw the Revolution. Narbonne, rendered unrecognizable, as much in his appearance as his accent, kept behind me, pretending to be indolent or sleepy, while I launched myself into the mysteries of politics.'

They crossed the Channel in three hours, speeded by a high wind – 'Narbonne brought up all he had eaten,' noted Bollman – and arrived in Dover at six in the evening of 20 August. From there they made their way to London where the Comtesse de la Châtre, an old friend of Narbonne's, welcomed them both to Talleyrand's house in Kensington Square where she was presiding in his absence.

Madame de Staël heard the news of their arrival on 26 August. 'You have saved my life and more than my life,' she wrote to Bollman, and to Narbonne in a letter breathless with relief: 'You do not know what dangers you have escaped. Those cruel men had sworn to destroy you, they claimed to have found papers which compromised you horribly, and totally unjustified though their accusations were, felt certain of being able to condemn you.'

In view of her pregnancy and the scandal it would cause if she arrived in England in such a condition without her husband, she would not be able to join Narbonne till after her baby was born. She planned to complete her pregnancy in Switzerland, where her parents had retired after her father's dismissal as Finance Minister in 1790. 'Write to me all the time,' she told Narbonne. 'Remember what a fearful sacrifice to duty I am making in separating myself from you.'

But though her passport to leave Paris had already been granted and though her parents awaited her anxiously in Switzerland, she lingered on in Paris, hating to leave while she could still save friends in danger. Narbonne was safe but there were two others to whom she

6

was specially attached. One of them, Mathieu, Vicomte de Montmorency Laval, bearer of one of the greatest names in France, had been the first of those noblemen who in a flush of altruism in 1789 had voted to abolish all hereditary honours. This democratic gesture had not sufficed to save him from the hatred of the Jacobins and he was now in hiding in the embassy. Idealistic and high-minded, he would remain her devoted follower all his life.

Charles Maurice de Talleyrand Périgord, former bishop of Autun, and the other object of her concern, was in less immediate danger. It had been he who proposed the confiscation of the Church's assets by the state in 1789 and as such still had some lingering credit with the left. He had spent the summer on a diplomatic mission to England and was now desperately seeking an official pretext to return there. Day by day he waited for his passport to be ratified by Danton; he would finally receive it on 7 September. Like Mathieu de Mont-morency he had probably been Madame de Staël's lover at one time. 'The three men I loved most in my youth,' she wrote years later, 'were N[arbonne], T[alleyrand], and M[ontmorency].' Though Narbonne had replaced the last two in her favours they kept a central place in her affections.

Less intimately linked, but dear to her as a friend and the lover of Madame de la Châtre, was François, Comte de Jaucourt, a former deputy and constitutionalist. Together with a fellow deputy, the Marquis de Lally Tollendal, he had been imprisoned in the Abbaye. Already there were rumours that a massacre was being planned for the Paris prisons. Lally Tollendal had a good chance of being released thanks to his friendship with Condorcet. Jaucourt had no such support. Running through the list of the members of the new Commune, whom she knew only by their terrible reputation, she chose the name of one, the public prosecutor, Pierre Louis Manuel. He had recently published an introduction to a collection of Mirabeau's letters, she remembered; as a *femme de lettres* herself she might perhaps win him by an appeal to his literary vanity.

Manuel gave her an appointment for seven the following morning. It was a somewhat democratic hour, she noted, but there was no question of being late. While she waited in Manuel's office she observed that he had a portrait of himself placed on his desk and began to hope that flattery would indeed prove the way to his heart. But Manuel, when he at last appeared, proved capable of listening to a genuine plea. Pointing out the appalling vicissitudes of revolutionary politics, she begged him to save Jaucourt and Lally Tollendal; perhaps one day he too would be imprisoned and the memory of his action would be a consolation. (He perished on the scaffold the following year.) That evening she received a note from him informing her that Jaucourt had been freed and that Condorcet had arranged for the release of Lally Tollendal.

It was now high time that she should leave Paris, but there was one last service to render. The Abbé de Montesquiou, a cousin of Narbonne's, was in imminent danger of arrest, and she had arranged that he should travel to Switzerland with her using the papers of a servant. A rendezvous had been arranged for the morning of 2 September. It was the first day of the September massacres in the prisons – the massacres that, in the words of Danton, put a 'river of blood' between the Revolution and its opponents. News of the fall of the frontier towns of Longwy and Verdun had just reached Paris; from early in the morning the alarm bells had been ringing as they had on 10 August. Madame de Staël had planned to leave Paris in as grand a style as possible, relying on the ambassadorial coach, with six men in livery, to underline her diplomatic status. She had scarcely left the embassy, however, when a swarm of 'hags from hell' fell on the coach, dragging the horses to a halt and crying that she was carrying off the nation's gold. A crowd quickly gathered and orders were given that she should be taken before the assembly of her local section, the Faubourg Saint Germain. With just time to whisper to a servant to warn the Abbé of what had happened, she was taken before the assembly and ordered to present herself at the Hôtel de Ville.

The journey to the Hôtel de Ville took over two hours. The coach was surrounded by a mob of people yelling for her blood – not that they knew her personally, she wrote, but the sight of a coach and livery was enough to rouse their fury. Looking back, she was astonished at the calm she felt. 'I realized,' she wrote to Narbonne, 'that the fear of death is as nothing beside a moment's anxiety on your behalf . . . "He is saved" were the words I kept repeating to myself like the Ave Marias of the faithful.'

Outside the Hôtel de Ville the steps were crowded by men with pikes. One of them lunged at her and, had he not been parried by the gendarme next to her, would have struck her to the ground. 'If I had fallen at that moment,' she wrote, 'it would have been all up with me; it is in the nature of the mob to respect what is upright; but when the victim has already fallen they finish him off.'

Inside the Hôtel de Ville Robespierre, with two secretaries, was presiding on a platform raised above a noisy crowd whose shouts of *'Vive la nation'* came near to drowning the proceedings. 'I breathed again at escaping the populace,' wrote Madame de Staël, 'but what a protector was Robespierre!' Half fainting, she was given a seat on the platform next to a slight acquaintance, the bailiff of Virieu; he rose to his feet on seeing her, declaring that he did not know her and that her affairs had nothing to do with him. 'The poor man's lack of chivalry displeased me,' she admitted, 'and I became all the more anxious to defend myself, seeing that he had no wish to spare me the trouble. I got up therefore and made plain the right I had to leave Paris as the ambassadress of Sweden, showing the passports which had been given to me in recognition of this fact.'

At this point Manuel arrived. Horrified at seeing her in such circumstances he made himself responsible for her, leading her and her maid to his office behind the hall. They stayed there for six hours, dying, she wrote, of hunger, thirst and fear. Through the window looking on to the Place de Grève they could see the mob returning from the prisons, their bare and bloodstained arms showing all too clearly what they had been doing. Inside the court suspicion that Madame de Staël had helped Narbonne to escape made the question of her immunity far from certain. Finally, for fear of provoking an incident with Sweden, it was decided to let her go. Late at night – he had not dared to risk his popularity by coming earlier – Manuel came to escort her home in her coach. The street was unlit, she wrote, but there were bands of men carrying torches whose light was far more frightening than the dark. From time to time their coach was stopped but Manuel's firm announcement that he was a member of the Commune brought them safely home.

The next day, with passports for herself and one servant, she was able to leave Paris. She scribbled a parting note to Madame de la

Châtre in England: 'Everything that interests my dear friend has been in perfect safety for the last two days. May this thought help her to bear the news [of the massacres] when she hears it. I leave in two hours.'

The secretary of the Commune, Tallien, who less than two years later would bring about the overthrow of Robespierre, had been deputed to escort her to the city gates. At every moment news came through of further killings in the prisons; outside the windows of the Temple the head of the Princesse de Lamballe was being paraded on a pike. A number of other fugitives, all highly compromised, were sheltering in the embassy when Tallien arrived. She begged him not to reveal their presence; in the event, though one of the most bloodthirsty of the Jacobins, he kept his promise not to do so.

'I climbed into the carriage with him,' she wrote. 'We parted without saying anything that was in our thoughts. Circumstances froze the words on our lips.' Four days later, after an uneventful journey, she arrived at the château of Coppet, her parents' house in Switzerland.

Chapter 2

Madame de Staël arrived in Switzerland to find herself something of a heroine. 'It had been established in Geneva as it had been in my part of Paris that I had been massacred with my maid on the steps of the Hôtel de Ville,' she wrote to Narbonne. 'As nothing could be closer to the truth I have been received by all Geneva with an interest that makes me think that should you wish it we could have a very pleasant refuge here.'

The memory of their parting haunted her. 'It was on the 19 August, at nine o'clock in the evening, that you left me to run the most horrible danger, that, finding a sort of courage in the firmness of my resolution, I was able to contemplate without dying those features which are so dear to me, telling myself that I might never see them again. Ah! I still held you in my arms, your heart still beat close to mine; in five months, to the hour, to the day, if I can, we will be reunited. Till then let the time pass quickly, let the leaves fall, let me give life to your child, and swear to its father that he is my angel, my saviour, the god of my idolatry.'

Meanwhile, in London, as news of the massacres came through and a flood of refugees poured in from France, Narbonne was doing his best to comfort Madame de la Châtre, still unaware of Jaucourt's release and hysterical with anxiety for her lover. Nothing could have been nobler than Narbonne's behaviour in this crisis, noted Bollman. Since their first dramatic meeting he had come to admire him more and more as a perfect product of the *ancien régime*, combining brilliant intellectual and social gifts with a simplicity and lack of self-assertion 'found only in those who know their own worth'. It was no wonder, he considered, that Madame de Staël preferred him to her husband who from all accounts 'could hardly invent a dish of potatoes'.

The news of Jaucourt's release and of Madame de Staël's safe arrival in Switzerland relieved Narbonne's most immediate anxieties. But there was little else to cheer him. Six months before he had been a minister, still trying to ride the tiger of the Revolution and to save the monarchy. In the short time at his disposal he had done his utmost to strengthen France's armies and defences and despite increasing polarization between left and right had briefly held the middle ground between them. Now he was a wanted man in France, denounced as a traitor in the National Convention, where he was accused of embezzling government funds while he was Minister of War. His property had been confiscated by the state and seals set on the doors of his Paris house. (Madame de Staël, foreseeing trouble, had been there earlier to rescue the most precious bronzes, books and wine.) His mother, wife and elder daughter were safe in Rome, attached to the household of the King's aunts, Mesdames Adelaide and Victoire, but his mother, indignant at his liberal politics, had broken off all relations with him. A younger daughter, two years old, had been left with her nurse in France; though so far unharmed, she was potentially at risk. The political aims and ambitions to which he had devoted himself for the last three years were in ruins. France had been declared a republic, the fate of the King aroused the gloomiest expectations. Having escaped death at the hands of the Jacobins he was greeted in London by the hatred of those ultra-royalist, or 'aristocratic' émigrés who had fled to England two years earlier and who held the constitutionalists responsible for the downfall of the monarchy.

Gradually, as September went by, the friends and allies of the constitutionalist party who had once formed the nucleus of Madame de Staël's salon in Paris made their way to London. Jaucourt was reunited with Madame de la Châtre, Lally Tollendal with his mistress of equally long standing, the Princesse d'Hénin. Mathieu de Montmorency followed not long after, to the intense relief of Madame de Staël, whose greatest regret had been at leaving him behind in Paris. Talleyrand, having at last received his passport, was not officially a refugee, but few believed the story that he had come to London on a mission to regularize weights and measures between England and France.

'Do not discuss me with the bishop,' wrote Madame de Staël to Narbonne, remembering her affair with Talleyrand, 'he is still too displeased that I am no longer under his spell . . . He may perhaps speak badly of me.'

In the great Whig houses of London, sympathetic to their progressive views, Narbonne and his friends were certain of a ready welcome. But they were regarded with suspicion by the Tory government and the authorities who saw them as carriers of dangerously subversive ideas and who kept a close eye on their movements. The King's suspension and imprisonment, the wave of arrests that followed, above all the horrors of the September massacres, had aroused a violent reaction in England. Those who had greeted the Revolution as the dawn of a new age were changing their tune. Never had public opinion been more conservative and royalist. The sturdy figure of George III, now happily restored to sanity, seemed a bulwark against the anarchy and bloodshed that were flourishing across the Channel.

As the political situation worsened in France, it seemed wisest for those most recently involved to withdraw as much as possible from public view. Talleyrand brazened out his unpopularity and continued to keep his finger on the pulse of events in London – on his earlier mission in the spring he had been shunned by society, while the Queen at a reception had deliberately turned her back on him. But other friends sought seclusion in the English countryside, away from the hostility they were bound to find in London. Lally Tollendal and the Princesse d'Hénin took a house in Richmond, then still entirely rural. Narbonne, with Madame de la Châtre, Jaucourt, Mathieu de Montmorency and others, went further afield to the Mickleham valley near Dorking in Surrey where they rented a house called Juniper Hall.

Juniper Hall, then as now, was a substantial red-brick mansion, tucked at the bottom of a wooded hill with gardens looking out across a view of fields and woods towards Box Hill; the cedars that shade the entrance today were only twelve years old in 1792. Once a coaching inn, it had been enlarged and remodelled in the 1750s, with a classical portico, tall arched windows and delicate plasterwork inside. Its crowning glory was the so-called sculptured drawing room, designed in the Adam manner by a gifted amateur artist, Lady Templeton. Exceptionally rich for its period, its walls were decorated with sculpted panels of classical scenes and figures, framed by lavish swags and garlands, a vision in white and gold and pastel colours, centring on a tall carved fireplace in grey and white marble.

To Narbonne and his companions, with the terrors of revolutionary Paris behind them, the house with its graceful decorations and rural setting must have seemed an idyllic place of refuge. The rent was largely subsidized by Madame de Staël, whose money orders to Narbonne under the assumed name of Sir John Glayre – all transfers to émigrés from France were blocked – helped keep the little community afloat. In a cottage at nearby Westhumble the Princesse de Broglie, recently arrived from France with her small son after fourteen hours in an open boat, set up house with another group of friends. Since the cottage was small, with poky, dirt-floored downstairs rooms, they dined most days at Juniper Hall, walking the mile or so between the two houses when it was fine or using the battered old cabriolet which was the colony's only form of transport when it rained.

To their Surrey neighbours the arrival of this distinguished group of refugees, freshly escaped from the dramas of the Revolution, and many of them leading actors in it, was a matter of absorbing interest. At Norbury Park, the grandest house in the vicinity, lived the family of William Lock, a rich and cultivated patron of the arts who numbered among his friends some of the leading artistic and intellectual figures of the day from the late lamented Dr Johnson to Fuseli and Thomas Lawrence. At the foot of the park lived Mrs Susanna Phillips, sister of the novelist Fanny Burney, and it is in a letter from Mrs Phillips to her sister in late September that the new arrivals are first announced:

'We shall shortly, I believe, have a little company of unfortunate (or rather fortunate, since here they are safe) French *noblesse* in our neighbourhood. Sunday evening Ravely [a neighbour] informed Mr Lock that two or three families had joined to take Jenkinson's house, Juniper Hall, and that another family had taken a small house at Westhumble, which the people very reluctantly let upon the Christian-like supposition that being nothing but French *papishes*, they would never pay.'

Mr Lock, she continued, had immediately sent word that he would be responsible for the rent though this had proved unnecessary. She had been gratified too to find that he intended to call on the two households, thus ensuring them the civility, at least, of their neighbours. 'I feel infinitely interested for all these persecuted persons,' she told her sister.

The daughter of the famous musicologist Charles Burney, Susanna Phillips had been an accomplished musician till marriage and the care of three small children had turned her energies elsewhere. Unlike her father and her sister Fanny, who were staunchly Tory in their views, she and her husband had welcomed the Revolution at its outset and had admired the liberalism of Narbonne and his fellow constitutionalists. She was filled with sympathy at the misfortunes that had overcome them and charmed when she met them by the gaiety and courage with which they faced their troubles. Since she spoke French fluently, having spent two years in Paris as a girl, she found conversation with them no problem and her letters, scattered with French phrases and expressions, give a lively impression of their first encounters.

'Mr Lock has been so kind as to pave the way for my introduction to Madame de la Châtre,' she wrote to her sister, 'and carried me on Friday to Juniper Hall where we found M. de Montmorency, a ci devant duc [sic], and one who gave some of the first examples of sacrificing personal interest to what was then considered public good. I know not whether you will like him better when I tell you that from him proceeded the motion for the abolition of titles in France; but if you do not, let me tell you in his excuse, that he was scarcely one and twenty when an enthusiastic spirit compelled him to this, I believe, ill judged and mischievous act.'

Madame de la Châtre received them with great politeness. 'She is about thirty three; an elegant figure, not pretty but with an animated and expressive countenance; very well read, *pleine d'esprit*, and, I think, very lively and charming.'

Narbonne came in soon after. 'He seems forty, rather fat but would be handsome were it not for a slight cast of one eye. He was this morning in great spirits. Poor man! It was the only time I have ever seen him so. He came up very courteously to me, and begged leave *de me faire sa cour* at Mickleham, to which I graciously assented.'

A new addition to the party was General Alexandre d'Arblay, formerly chief of staff to Lafayette, and one of Narbonne's greatest friends. He had been arrested with his commander when Lafayette, having failed to rally the army to the King, had fled to the Austrian camp; while Lafayette would be imprisoned for five years by the Austrians, those of his staff who, like d'Arblay, had taken no part in politics had been released and allowed to proceed to Holland. There Narbonne had written to him. '*Et comme il l'aime infiniment*,' said Madame de la Châtre, '*il l'a prié de venir vivre avec lui.*'

The chief of staff to Lafayette, a hero to those who had welcomed the first stages of the Revolution, could not fail to be of interest to Mrs Phillips. She found him a 'true *militaire, franc et loyal*', tall, with a good figure and an open manly countenance. She was delighted when he came to call soon after.

'Phillips was at work in the parlour and I had just stepped into the next room . . . when I heard a man's voice and presently distinguished these words: "*Je ne parle pas trop bien l'Anglais, monsieur.*" I came forward immediately to relieve Phillips and then found it was M. d'Arblay.'

She took him upstairs to the drawing room, the children capering before them. '*Ah, madame!*' cried d'Arblay, '*la jolie petite maison que vous avez et les jolis petits hôtes!*' He took her small son Norbury on his knee and played with him. 'I asked him,' wrote Mrs Phillips, 'if he were not proud of being so kindly noticed by the adjutant general of M. Lafayette. "*Est ce qu'il sait le nom de M. Lafayette?*" said he smiling. I said he was our hero. "*Ah! nous voilà donc bons amis! Il n'y a pas de plus brave homme sur terre!*" "*Et comme on l'a traité!*" cried I. A little shrug and his eyes cast up was the only answer.'

They talked of Lafayette and his imprisonment, Mrs Phillips

lamenting the downfall of one who at the outset of the Revolution had been the most popular man in France.

'This led M. d'Arblay to speak of M. de Narbonne to whom I found him passionately attached,' she wrote. 'Upon my mentioning the sacrifices made by the French nobility, many of them voluntarily, he said no one had made more than M. de Narbonne; that, previous to the Revolution, he had more wealth and power than almost any except the Princes of the Blood.'

Speaking of his own fortune – 'something immense, but I never remember the number of hundred thousand livres' – he told her he had lost everything.

'And now Madame, you see me reduced to nothing save a little ready money and little enough of that. What Narbonne may be able to save from the ruins of his fortune I cannot tell, but whatever it is we will share it together. I haven't the slightest scruple about this, since we've always made common cause together and love one another like brothers.'

'I wish I could paint the manly *franchise* with which these words were spoken,' concluded Mrs Phillips, 'but you will not find it surprising that they raised MM de Narbonne and d'Arblay very high in my estimation.'

A few days later it was Narbonne's turn to call, bringing two volumes of Marmontel's newly-published *Contes Moraux*. There must have been something immediately sympathetic about Mrs Phillips – her portraits show a delicate, pretty face with great sweetness of expression – for he too settled down to talk with her at length.

'He was in very depressed spirits, I saw,' she wrote, 'and entered into some details of his late situation with great frankness . . . Last May *il donna sa démission* of the place of Ministre de la Guerre, being annoyed in all his proceedings by the Jacobins, and prevented from serving his country effectively by the instability of the King for whom he nonetheless professes a sincere attachment. "But it was impossible for me to serve him – he was the same to all his greatest friends, both in his virtues and his defects . . . he had no faith in himself and in consequence distrusted everybody else."'

Susanna's relationship to Fanny Burney was a source of lively curiosity to her new acquaintances. They discovered it, she told her sister, 'without my assistance'.

'Mad^e de Broglie speaking of English books wth wch she was acquainted I believe on Mrs Lock's first visit, named *Evelina* and *Cecilia*; & thus induced Mrs Lock to mention the Author's Sister, a certain Mad^e Phillips, as one of her friends . . . This acc^t travell'd from Mad^e de Broglie to Mad^e de la Châtre and from her to the Gentlemen.'

She was plied with questions next time she visited Juniper Hall.

'It's said that your sister was prodigiously young when she wrote *Evelina*.'

'That is true, Monsieur.'

'And is it also true, as people say, that she wrote the novel to amuse Monsieur your father when he was ill?'

'Oh no, Monsieur, nothing could be further from the truth, since the book was published several months before my father had the slightest idea of its existence.'

And Susanna recounted briefly the story of *Evelina*'s anonymous publication, the growing chorus of praise, her sister's emergence as a famous author at the age of twenty-five.

To Madame de Staël, installed with her parents in Switzerland and wearily awaiting her baby's birth, Juniper Hall seemed as distant and alluring as the promised land. 'My soul is there already,' she told Narbonne. She fretted and chafed at her separation from her lover, not least because Narbonne, preoccupied by his country's misfortunes, was not always a conscientious correspondent. She accused him of heartlessness, of cruelty more terrible than the Jacobins', when he failed to write; she swore that his neglect would bring about her death in childbirth.

His letters, when they did arrive, brought an instant lift of spirits. 'The gods who at the end of every opera in the world restore the heroine to life do not produce such a sudden transformation as the sight of your letters does to me,' she wrote. Her sufferings assuaged, she was able to turn to more mundane subjects, to tell him of the progress of their first child Auguste, now two (and officially the child of Baron de Staël), and to complain of the difficulties of living with her parents. Her father, Jacques Necker, was in reality too doting a parent to cross his only daughter though he deplored her liaison, but her mother, Bible in hand, preached sermons at her day and night. The projected arrival of her husband in Switzerland posed further problems. It would come, she noted, at a very difficult time for her since the baby she was expecting was due ten months from the time she had last seen him. Then, too, he would caress Auguste as though he were his son and she felt sickened at the very thought.

To console herself she had turned to writing and was composing an extended essay, *De l'Influence des passions sur le bonheur des individus et des nations*, which, published four years later, would reflect the turmoil of emotions she was experiencing. And since it was scarcely less possible to her not to take an interest in politics than not to breathe, she was following events in France with passionate attention.

Since the middle of August the King and the royal family had been imprisoned in the Temple. The trial of the King for so-called crimes against the nation was due to take place in early December. From his refuge in Switzerland, his presence there only grudgingly tolerated by the authorities, Jacques Necker was engaged in writing a defence of the King which would be printed and delivered to the National Convention. Madame de Staël sent a copy to her lover at Juniper Hall, where it was eagerly scanned and discussed by the little colony, but privately she expressed her misgivings that her father's gesture might lead to reprisals against him in France and the confiscation of his property there. She blamed the desire for glory (or, in modern terms, publicity) which led her father to publish his defence – any threat to her father's fortune was a threat to her own, and thus to her joint future with Narbonne.

Narbonne, lordly about his own and other people's money, was far from descending to such considerations. From the moment the question of the King's trial had been raised he had been plunged into a state of intense agitation. Even before the sacking of the Tuileries on 10 August he had been involved with Madame de Staël in a plan to arrange the royal family's escape from Paris – the King, suspicious of the constitutionalists, had refused their help. Now, feeling his honour engaged and acutely sensitive to the accusations of the royalist émigrés that the policies he had pursued had brought the King to this pass, he was doing everything in his power to come to his defence. In London he sought out his former ministerial colleagues, proposing that they should demand a joint safe conduct to France in order to take their part in meeting the charges against the King.

Failing to get their agreement (on the grounds that the trial was not legal), he wrote directly to the National Convention demanding the right to give evidence for the King as former Minister of War – the King was accused, amongst other things, of having contributed to France's military defeats by hindering the army's preparations and being in contact with the enemy. At the same time he was doing all he could to muster English opinion in favour of an intervention on the King's behalf, hurrying up to London to canvass his friends amongst the Whigs and even obtaining an interview with the Tory Prime Minister, William Pitt. His pleas were heard in glacial silence. 'For no consideration in the world,' Pitt told him finally, 'can England expose herself by pleading in vain on such a subject and before such men.'

Fortunately for her peace of mind, Madame de Staël knew nothing of her lover's *démarche*. Her greatest anxiety was that during the King's trial Narbonne should not show his face in England where he would be exposed to all the fury of the royalist émigrés. She insisted vehemently that he should remain at Juniper Hall, away from the public eye, and that he should make no move that would draw attention to himself. The fact that he was doing just the opposite was spared her till after her baby was born.

Chapter 3

On 20 November Madame de Staël gave birth to a son. 'Behold me mother of the Gracchi,' she wrote to the historian Edward Gibbon. 'I hope my two sons will restore liberty in France.' Gibbon, once her mother's suitor and now a family friend, was living in Lausanne and might, thought Madame de Staël, be a useful ally in obtaining permission from the authorities for her lover and her friends eventually to take refuge there.

In the meantime, all her thoughts were turned to England, where she intended to spend the next few months. Her children could be left with her parents. Despite their scenes and protests, she was determined to go there as soon as she was recovered. Already there were rumours of war between France and Britain. 'The earth trembles on all sides,' she told Gibbon, 'and if I do not make haste an abyss will open between my friend and me.'

Still convalescing and counting the days to her departure, Madame de Staël was thrown into new and convulsive agitation when on 2 December she heard of her lover's demand to appear at the trial of the King. The safe conduct he had asked for would be worthless. In exposing his life to danger, she considered, Narbonne was deliberately sacrificing hers. She had no patience with the motives of chivalry and honour which had inspired him; the desire to be noticed and talked about, she was convinced, had carried more weight than the hope of being useful.

'If you set foot in France,' she declared dramatically, 'I shall instantly blow out my brains. Go ahead if you must but remember as you take your first step on French soil that you trample beneath you a heart that has beaten only for you. Farewell!'

The news that the National Convention had refused Narbonne's demand to give evidence brought some relief of her worst fears. But echoes of the shock she had received reverberated through her letters. She was only twenty-five, she told him – in fact she was twenty-six – but she sensed she had not long to live. She begged him to remain at Juniper Hall, to do nothing till her arrival. 'Spare me these final days – let me descend in peace to the grave you have prepared for me.' As she made her plans to cross Europe her fear of her lover's quixotry revived. Though her diplomatic status should be enough to protect her, it was just possible she might be arrested. Any attempt on his part to come to France to help her, she told him, would deal her a mortal blow; it would destroy not only him but her. Such fears, she knew, were close to folly. But her head was turning with the anguish he had caused her, with the reproaches of her parents, with the possibility of her husband's arrival in Switzerland before she left. 'I think when I get to England my first stop will be Bedlam.'

It is probable that Narbonne awaited her arrival with mixed feelings. In England the passing of a bill requiring all French citizens to register as aliens, and authorizing their expulsion should it be thought necessary, made the position of the constitutionalists increasingly insecure. A year later Talleyrand would be expelled under the terms of this Aliens bill. Madame de Staël's arrival without her husband would be bound to attract adverse publicity. To the royalist émigrés she was a hated and notorious figure; their malice might well work against her with the British authorities.

This embarrassment apart, the extravagance of his mistress's devotion, her adoration as well as her reproaches, was beginning to weigh on Narbonne. For three years his life had been politically linked with hers. The influence of her father, Jacques Necker, had been a powerful first attraction; later she had been a dynamic motivating force during his period as Minister of War, writing, intriguing and inspiring others on his behalf. Perhaps under the spell of her enthusiasm he had let himself be carried further than he wished. The King was his godfather and possibly a closer relation still; his whole code as a soldier and a nobleman enforced the idea of loyalty to the crown. As the trial of the King continued and all hopes of saving him receded, his thoughts were far more with his monarch than his mistress.

In Surrey Narbonne's neighbours had been following the trial and his attempts to testify with sympathy and concern.

'Everything that is most shocking, may, I fear, be expected for the unfortunate King of France, his Queen and almost all that belong to them,' wrote Mrs Phillips to Fanny Burney. 'M. d'Arblay said it would indeed scarce have been possible to hope that M. de Narbonne could have escaped with his life had the *sauf conduit* requested been granted him.'

'But,' d'Arblay told her, 'he ardently wished to serve the King; he even considered his honour involved, and in such a case – *ma foi!* – one does not fear death. But since he is to be allowed no defenders, and such depths of atrocity have been reached, I shall never again set foot in France.'

'But isn't it always possible that things could change?' said Mr Lock.

'I'm sorry, Monsieur, but I see no hope of tranquillity for my unhappy country in my lifetime. The people have been so vitiated by seeing crimes committed with impunity, so accustomed to bloodshed and every kind of disorder, that as far as I can see there'll be neither peace nor security in France for the next thirty or forty years.

'Luckily for us,' he added more cheerfully, 'you have adopted us, and I hope we'll never leave you.'

Since their first meetings Mrs Phillips had seen much of Narbonne, d'Arblay and their fellow refugees. Her cottage on the outskirts of Mickleham was in easy walking distance of Juniper Hall. Norbury Park, at the summit of a wooded hill above the village, made the third point of a triangle. The Phillipses and the Locks were the dearest of friends; both households took the Juniper Hall colony to their hearts. Witty and cultivated, touched as they were by the glamour of great events, the little group shone brightly in contrast to the country gentry of the neighbourhood. Mrs Lock had always found her neighbours rather dull and tended to avoid them when she could.

Norbury Park, nonetheless, was a landmark in the neighbourhood. It had been built by her husband, William Lock, some twenty years before. Its site, at the top of Norbury Hill, gave it a view across the downs that stretched for miles. The woods that surrounded it were of well-established beech and oak, and the famous Druids Grove of ancient yews which lay a short walk from the house was a place of local legend. The house itself was a handsome building in the Palladian style, with a pillared hall and grand saloon whose walls were painted with romantic landscape scenes, torrents, crags and mountains, to complement the view outside; the carpet, to complete the illusion, was green to carry the eye to the lawn beyond. Here, under the hospitable eye of their host, the Juniper Hall colony could forget their troubles for a while, or at least discuss them in a sympathetic atmosphere.

Mrs Phillips, in the rambling, journalistic letters she was accustomed to exchange with her sister, gives vivid glimpses of these occasions and less formal encounters at her cottage and Juniper Hall. Let us follow her, with her husband, Captain Molesworth Phillips, on one of their first visits to their neighbours:

Tuesday, 27 November. – Phillips and I determined at about half past one to walk to *Junipère* together.

M. d'Arblay received us at the door and showed the most flattering degree of pleasure at our arrival.

We found with Madame de la Châtre another French gentleman, M. Siccard, who was also an officer of M. Lafayette's.

M. de Narbonne said he hoped we would be sociable and dine with them now and then. Madame de la Châtre made a speech to the same effect. '*Et quel jour, par exemple,*' said M. de Narbonne, '*ferait mieux qu'aujourd'hui?*' Madame de la Châtre took my hand instantly to press in the most pleasing and gratifying manner imaginable this proposal; and before I had time to answer, M. d'Arblay, snatching up his hat, declared he would run and fetch the children.

I was obliged to entreat Phillips to bring him back and entreated him to *entendre raison.*

'*Mais, mais, Madame!*' cried M. de Narbonne, '*ne soyez pas disgracieuse.*'

'*Je ne suis pas disgracieuse,*' answered I, *assez naïvement,* which occasioned a general comical but not affronting laugh: '*sur ce sujet au moins,*' I had the modesty to add. I pleaded their late hour of dinner, our having no carriage and my disuse of the night air at this time of year; but M. de Narbonne said their cabriolet (they have no other carriage) should take us home, and that there was a top to it, and Madame de la Châtre declared she would cover me well with shawls, etc.

'*Allons, allons,*' cried M. d'Arblay; '*voilà qui est fait, car je parie que Monsieur Phillips n'aura pas le courage de nous refuser.*'

Effectivement, Monsieur Phillips was perfectly agreeable: so that all my efforts were in vain, and I was obliged to submit, in despite of various worldly scruples, to pass a most charmingly pleasant day.

And here is d'Arblay calling in one morning to find the Phillipses in the midst of tidying up.

'He almost scolded me,' wrote Mrs Phillips, 'for wanting to put away some of Phillips' scattered garments which were lying about – "*Enfin*, Mad^e Philippe" s^d he, "I'll put on airs too – I won't come and see you any more except in white silk stockings – – I've only got three pairs – in consequence I won't be able to come very often!"

'I believe he will force me to mind him no more than I sh^ld mind James [her brother] if he lived in the village.'

For all the affability of her new friends, Mrs Phillips had no illusions about the regrets and anxieties which beset them. She listened to them talk one day of France's hard-won liberty.

'Bah,' said a guest, the Marquis de Girardin, 'do you call that liberty?'

'But they will have it,' said Jaucourt, 'and what angers me most is that they won't allow me to speak well of it; they have ruined the cause.'

Across the Channel the revolutionary army had thrown back the invading enemy and was advancing into Belgium; the resounding victories of Valmy and Jemappes had reversed the disasters of the summer months. There was a bitter satisfaction in their country's victories; Talleyrand called on the French ambassador in London to offer his congratulations. But the political news from France was grim. The number of arrests was mounting; the mood of the National Convention was moving sharply leftwards. The trial of the King was proceeding, inevitably it seemed, towards a fatal conclusion. Narbonne, unable to appear as a witness, had published his own defence of the King, denouncing his accusers and confirming, from his own experiences as Minister of War, the King's zeal for the interests of the nation. His depression, indeed near-desperation, over the King's fate struck Mrs Phillips painfully. Much moved, she listened to him read Necker's *Défense du Roi* with emotion and '*beaucoup d'âme*'.

The King had behaved with singular ingratitude to both Narbonne and d'Arblay, Jaucourt told Mrs Phillips privately, and had dismissed Narbonne because he could not trust him with his counter-revolutionary plans. As for d'Arblay, he had been the officer on guard at the time of the royal family's flight to Varennes, and having been kept in perfect ignorance of their intentions, had narrowly escaped being massacred when the flight was discovered.

Meanwhile the other members of their circle had suffered a fresh blow with the decree of the National Convention denouncing as émigrés not only those royalists who had left France voluntarily, often to fight in the army of the Princes (Louis XVI's brothers, the Comtes d'Artois and Provence), but those who had been forced to flee for their lives after 10 August. Unless they returned to register their residence in France within three months all their property would be forfeit to the state and those who returned thereafter would be liable to the death penalty. 'Ma'am,' said Mr Clarke, the tutor whom Narbonne had engaged to teach the Juniperians English, 'it reduces this family to nothing; all they can hope is, by the help of their parents and friends, to get together the wherewithal to purchase a cottage in America and live as they can.'

Calling to condole next day, Mrs Phillips found Jaucourt at least prepared to joke about his misfortunes:

'I think I may have a slight vocation for cooking; I shall make myself a cook. Do you know what our cook said to us this morning? He was consulting me on the dangers he would run in returning to France. "However, monsieur," he said, "there's an exception [in the new law] for *artists*." I shall be an artist cook as well.'

Narbonne and d'Arblay, already dispossessed in France, had no hope of recovering their property. But Mathieu de Montmorency and others, preferring to risk 'the daggers of Marat' rather than face perpetual banishment and the loss of all their possessions, determined to undertake the perilous journey to France. The Princesse de Broglie and Madame de la Châtre followed not long after, taking refuge in Boulogne where the mayor, sympathetic to the constitutionalists, had promised to protect them. Jaucourt, faithful to Madame de la Châtre, went with her, though, too discreet to spell out their relationship, he told his Surrey neighbours that he was going to France in order to save his sister's property from confiscation.

Narbonne and those left behind at Juniper Hall watched the departure of their friends with foreboding. On the evening after Madame de la Châtre left England, they were dining with the Locks at Norbury Park when Narbonne was called to the front hall where someone was enquiring for him. He returned a few minutes later with a travel-worn man in a greatcoat whom he introduced to Mrs Lock as the Comte de la Châtre. After three years apart, and every kind of misfortune on his journey across Europe, including the loss of all his luggage in a shipwreck, he had arrived a day too late to find his wife.

This *coup de théâtre* threw the party into stupefaction. But la Châtre, a perfectly complaisant husband, seemed cheerful enough as, once the introductions had been made, he stood warming his back by the fire and talking to Narbonne. The two men had not met since the outset of the Revolution, when each had followed very different paths, Narbonne a constitutionalist, la Châtre a diehard royalist who had been fighting with the army of the Princes till its disbandment some weeks earlier. They rallied each other good-humouredly on their misfortunes, la Châtre making fun of *ses amis les constitutionnaires*, Narbonne riposting gaily on the party of the Princes.

'*Eh bien*,' said la Châtre, '*chacun à son tour* – you were the first to be ruined – you made a constitution that wouldn't hold.'

'*Pardon*,' cried d'Arblay quickly, 'but it was never tried.'

'*Eh bien*, it fell through all the same – there's no question of it any more,' said la Châtre. 'Now we can all starve merrily together.'

Narbonne assured him gravely that he still had a few bottles of wine and that while he stayed with him he should not be reduced to drinking beer.

Madame de Staël, in Switzerland, was in no mood to take her troubles so light-heartedly. Her parents' reproaches, she told Narbonne, were driving her to the brink of suicide. She had answered all their protests with a single ultimatum: she would either go to England or to the bottom of the lake. The departure of Madame de la Châtre was a further aggravation. She had been relying on her presence to preserve appearances while she was at Juniper Hall. She hoped Narbonne would find some other lady to keep her countenance. 'Do try and seduce one for me,' she wrote, 'as long as she doesn't please you too much.' But with or without this sop to convention, she was now poised to leave Switzerland.

'The time has come,' she told her lover, 'to choose between you and the rest of the world, and it is to you that my heart bids me turn. May the gift of my life embellish yours, may I never become devalued in your eyes by the very sacrifices I am making to my passion for you. Even if my reputation is damaged for ever may you never think less of the woman who has recognized no law but love!'

Shortly before Christmas, in order to avoid a final scene with her parents, she announced that she was going to visit friends in Geneva. Instead she set out on the journey to England, pausing just outside Paris, at Passy, where Mathieu de Montmorency was to meet her and escort her to the boat at Boulogne. 'There's no need to hide from you,' wrote her father to a friend, 'how deeply this journey distresses me. I have done everything in my power to prevent it but to no avail.' As for Narbonne, bound by gratitude and his continuing obligations to the woman who had saved his life, there was nothing to be done but to wait for her arrival with as good a grace as possible.

Chapter 4

'**M**y dearest Susanna's details of the French Colony at Juniper are truly interesting,' wrote Fanny Burney to her sister. Though she disapproved of their progressive politics, she sympathized with their misfortunes and since, far more than Mrs Phillips, she moved in the great world she promised to do what she could to influence opinion in their favour. It would be a difficult task, she told her, 'especially as *All* the *Constituents* are now reviled as authors and originators of the misfortunes of France, from their arrogant self-sufficiency in their powers to *stop*, as well as begin, when they pleased.'

Their plight, she considered, was an example to all would-be reformers in Britain. 'New Systems, I fear in States, are always dangerous, if not wicked. Grievance by grievance, wrong by wrong, must only be assailed, & breathing time allowed to old prejudices, & old habits, between all that is done.'

Fanny Burney, in a very different way, had only recently emerged from exile herself. For five years she had been Second Keeper of the Robes to the Queen, confined by the rigorous and wearisome regime of the Court, her talents wasted, as Horace Walpole put it, in the folding of muslins. What had been welcomed as an honour when the post was first offered had proved to be a burden which had almost

30

destroyed her health. It was only at the insistence of her friends and family that she at last plucked up the courage to offer her resignation. By this time her health was close to collapse, and a long period of convalescence followed her departure from the Court. She remained devoted to the Queen, however, and a pension of £100 a year was a reward for her years of service. 'It is but her due,' said George III good-naturedly; 'she has given up five years of her pen.'

The return to her family and a more leisured life eventually restored Fanny Burney's health and spirits. But her years at Court had left their mark. Her diaries preserve for posterity, with all the liveliness and humour of her first novel *Evelina*, a gallery of characters at Court, from the poor bewildered King in his first attack of madness to the overbearing Mrs Schwellenberg, her fellow Keeper of the Robes. But in public she had grown more circumspect. Celebrity had made her cautious. 'I would a thousand times rather forfeit my character as an author,' she wrote primly, 'than risk ridicule or censure as a female.' The spontaneous gaiety and fun of *Evelina* were already more muted in her second novel *Cecilia*. The years at Court would deepen this effect. As a former member of the royal household she must avoid the slightest breath of impropriety.

Fanny Burney was now forty, small, brown-haired, neat-featured, with a face and figure far more youthful than her years. She had suffered more than one disappointment in love, most recently at Court where a fellow courtier who had shown her marked attention had thrown her over in favour of a younger heiress. Fanny's books had enriched no one but her publisher. Without private means or aristocratic connections, she would never be loved for anything but herself. Deeply affectionate, she found her chief consolation amongst her large and lively family and in the company of a few close friends, Mrs Lock of Norbury Park among them.

It was on a visit to Mrs Lock, with whom she went to stay towards the end of January 1793, that Fanny Burney first met the French neighbours about whom she had heard so much. She found them in a state of utter consternation. On 20 January Louis XVI had been condemned to death; on the following day the sentence had been carried out. The news struck England like a thunderbolt; theatres were closed, the Court and Parliament went into mourning. Fanny herself, writing hastily for a suitable dress from home, was ashamed to venture out in anything but black.

Her first letters from Norbury Park are full of her shock and horror at the death of the King, and of the anguish it had occasioned at Juniper Hall. Narbonne and d'Arblay had been almost annihilated, she told her father. 'They are forever repining that they are French and though two of the most accomplished & elegant men I ever saw, they break our hearts with the humiliation they feel for their guiltless BIRTH in that guilty country. – "*Est-ce vrai*," cries M. de Narbonne, "*que vous conservez encore quelque amitié, M. Lock, pour ceux qui ont la honte et le malheur d'être nés français?*" Poor man! – He has all the symptoms upon him of the Jaundice – and M. d'Arblay, from a very fine figure and good face, was changed, as if by magic, in one night, upon the receipt of this inexpiable news, into an appearance as black, as meagre, & as miserable as M. de la Blancherie.'

It was at this moment of tragedy that Madame de Staël arrived in England. The longed-for reunion with her lover was shadowed with deepest gloom. The shock which all emigrants experienced at the death of the King was compounded for the constitutionalists by the fear that their policies, by undermining the throne, had indeed been partly responsible. For Narbonne the crisis of conscience would be profound.

'Alas,' wrote Madame de Staël soon after their first meeting, 'the pain you were feeling wrung my heart. The expression on your face, the efforts you were making to master your emotions sounded a grievous echo in my soul. Forgive me for loving you so much that I see pain, like happiness, in you alone.'

To d'Arblay, as Narbonne's closest friend, she turned for help in rousing him from his depression, and d'Arblay, almost equally distressed, did his best to interpret his friend's feelings, his loyalty to the principles of the Revolution, his horror at the crimes committed in their name. His memorandum of the conversation, preserved amongst the Burney papers, would be annotated in Fanny Burney's hand: '*Ample sujet à des réflexions les plus sérieuses.*'

Meanwhile, whatever her private concerns, Madame de Staël's position as an ambassadress, travelling without her husband, required explanation – the Aliens bill could otherwise cause problems. She hastened to justify her presence with a letter to the Foreign Secretary, Lord Grenville. The revulsion with which France inspired her, she wrote, had made it impossible for her to remain on its dishonoured soil a moment longer. Unable to wait for her husband to accompany her, she had sought refuge in England, 'that glorious country thanks to whose virtues it is still possible to believe in the benefits of true liberty'; despite her unwillingness to talk of her own concerns, her husband's diplomatic status made it necessary to inform him of this move. 'It is wise to cover oneself diplomatically,' she told Narbonne. Lally Tollendal, with whom she had spent her first night in England, backed her up with a less formal letter to the Foreign Secretary, warning him not to be influenced by the malice which the royalist émigrés would undoubtedly show towards her. He had seen her weep bitterly at the death of the King; she had been far more affected by the catastrophe than many of those who criticized her.

Despite the tragic circumstances surrounding her arrival, Madame de Staël's appearance at Juniper Hall brought a breath of new life, generous and inspiriting, to the saddened company. 'She is a woman of the first abilities, I think, I have ever seen,' wrote Fanny Burney to her father soon after meeting her. 'She is more in the style of Mrs Thrale than of any other celebrated Character; but she has infinitely more depth, & seems an even *profound* politician & metaphysician.' She described to her father Madame de Staël's heroic conduct in saving Narbonne and other friends in the days preceding the September massacres. From a letter the ambassadress had received from Paris she was able to recount details of the King's last moments – the little Dauphin's pathetic plea to be allowed to beg for his father's life before the National Convention, the despairing shrieks of his family as the King was taken from the Temple to his execution, the Abbé Edgeworth's famous farewell words: '*Fils de Saint Louis, montez au ciel!*'

Narbonne, she reported, had been quite ill with grief, but a letter from Malesherbes, the King's defence lawyer, had brought him some consolation. In it Malesherbes (who would be guillotined himself the following year) described how touched the King had been by Narbonne's letter on his behalf. Scrupulous to the last, he had recommended that it should not be used, for fear of compromising Narbonne even further.

Like a magnet, the presence of Madame de Staël drew company to Juniper Hall: Beaumetz, Malouet, the Lameth brothers, all friends and colleagues from her Paris days. Talleyrand arrived on an extended visit, perhaps to try his luck again with his old friend, at any rate to enjoy the pleasures of good company and conversation. For the brilliant and witty society of pre-revolutionary Paris conversation had almost been the reason for existence; the lack of it in exile was a deprivation even worse than poverty.

Fanny Burney was no stranger to good conversation. She had been the darling of Dr Johnson, she had moved in a society which included such figures as Sheridan, Burke and Garrick. But she was soon as dazzled as her sister by the charms of the Juniper Hall colony. Her political prejudices melted in their company. Narbonne, for all his underlying melancholy, was a delightful conversationalist – graceful, witty, infinitely quick in repartee. 'You could not keep your Heart from him if you saw him only for half an Hour,' wrote Fanny, perhaps rather optimistically, to her father, for his Tory views were deeply entrenched. Of Talleyrand, the former bishop, 'that viper who has cast his skin', as Horace Walpole described him, she was at first more doubtful. Pallid, limping, preceded by his reputation as a renegade and cynic, he inspired her with instinctive distrust.

'How do you like him?' whispered Madame de Staël when she first met him.

'Not very much,' answered Fanny, 'but then I do not know him.'

'Oh, I assure you,' cried Madame de Staël, '*he is the best of the men.*'

Before long Fanny Burney was forced to agree. 'It is inconceivable what a convert M. de Talleyrand has made of me,' she wrote; 'I think him now one of the first members & one of the most charming, of this exquisite set: Susanna is equally a prosylite. His powers of entertainment are astonishing, both in information & in raillery.'

But it was General d'Arblay, so frank and open that it was difficult to believe he was not English, who made the most impression on her. With all his soldierly virtues, she told her father, he was passionately fond of literature, well versed in German and Italian, and a most elegant poet. 'He has just undertaken to become my French master, for pronunciation, & he gives me long daily lessons in reading. Pray expect wonderful improvements!'

In return, Fanny Burney had promised to teach d'Arblay English; each evening they exchanged themes or compositions in the other's language to be corrected and returned.

'How M^e de S[taël] has she appeared to you?' asked d'Arblay in his opening theme; 'is it not true that this charming lady has a very uncommon character? great many parts, good spirits and the most rare indulgence?'

He was writing in the painted drawing room at Norbury Park. Fanny was upstairs in her room.

'Why don't you get down?' he asked her, 'every body in the drawing room calls after you. Some thought you were gone to Darking. Some others you had got a Sittkness; at last — M. de Narbonne was affraid to finding you low spirited, and all the society schew an uneasiness wich I have desired to put an end.'

Fanny Burney would preserve these themes and her replies, the start of a gradually unfolding love affair, as a precious record of their first acquaintance. Madame de Staël, always alive to emotional nuances, watched the relationship with interest. She had been immediately drawn to Fanny Burney, whose fame as a novelist extended far beyond the British Isles. Indeed, as she told her, she owed her a debt of gratitude, for her father Jacques Necker had fallen into a state of utter dejection at the time of Louis XVI's trial. Fanny's novel *Cecilia*, which someone had put into his hands, had 'soothed and regaled' him at a time when nothing else could move or touch him. 'I own I was not *very* much displeased at this,' wrote Fanny to her father.

Madame de Staël's admiration for Fanny Burney was unfeigned. Her own best novels, with their background of European politics and ideas, still lay ahead. But Fanny Burney, first in *Evelina* and then in *Cecilia*, had broken entirely new ground as a novelist of domestic life, finding her material in the society she saw around her and in the everyday incidents that any young woman, just entering the world, might encounter. Her novels opened the way for Jane Austen and a host of women writers after. Jane Austen's admiration for her is well known.

"'And what are you reading, Miss — ?'" she wrote in *Northanger Abbey*. "'Oh! it is only a novel,' replies that young lady while she lays down her book with affected indifference or momentary shame. "It is only *Cecilia* or *Camilla** . . ." or in short only some work in which the greatest powers of the mind are displayed, in which the most thorough knowledge of human nature, the happiest delineation of its varieties, the liveliest effusions of wit and humour, are conveyed to the world in the best chosen language.'

Madame de Staël had an eye for excellence. Throughout her life she would be surrounded by the best and liveliest spirits of the age. It was no wonder that she should cultivate Fanny Burney; in the somewhat equivocal circumstances of her stay at Juniper Hall, the friendship of the older woman, a famous writer and a former member of the royal household, had obvious practical advantages too. She made much of it in a letter to Gibbon (which she knew would be passed on to her parents). Fanny Burney, she wrote, had taken a romantic fancy to her as a fellow writer and 'bluestocking'.

Fanny would not have denied it. The warmth of the ambassadress's interest, her brilliance and her vitality, had swept her off her feet. Looking back on their friendship years later, she compared her once again to Mrs Thrale. Madame de Staël, by then a European figure, might well have questioned the comparison:

'They had the same sort of highly superior intellect, the same depth of learning . . . the same buoyant animal spirits such as neither sickness, sorrow, or even terror could subdue . . . Both had a fund inexhaustible of good humour and sportive gaiety . . . and though not either of them had the smallest real malevolence in their compositions, neither of them could withstand the pleasure of uttering a repartee, let it wound whom it might . . . Both were kind, charitable and munificent and therefore beloved; both were sarcastic, careless and daring and therefore feared. The morality of Madame de Staël was by far the most faulty but so was that of the society in which she lived.'

For the time being, however, Fanny Burney was blissfully

*Fanny Burney's third novel, published in 1796

unaware of the morality, faulty or otherwise, of her new friends at Juniper Hall. 'There can be nothing imagined more charming, more fascinating than this Colony,' she told her father. 'Between their Sufferings & their *agrémens* they occupy us almost wholly.'

Chapter 5

————— ⌒≫⌒ —————

E arly in February the Locks left Norbury Park for London, where they had taken a house in Portland Place and where their eldest daughters, Augusta and Amelia, aged seventeen and fifteen, hoped to enjoy the pleasures of the London season. They were greatly missed by their French neighbours, who had come to look on Mr Lock, at nearly sixty, as something of a sage and mentor. Pretty Fredy Lock, considerably younger than her husband, her melting ways a contrast to his more solid intellectual qualities, was equally missed. With their numerous children, from twenty-four-year-old William downwards, they made an idyllic if somewhat sentimental picture of English family life. Dr Burney, who found its sweetness rather cloying, used to complain of the 'viscosity' of his daughters' relations with the Locks.

Fanny Burney stayed on in Surrey at her sister's cottage. Captain Phillips was away on a recruiting mission; it was a pleasure to have her sister and her children to herself. She went to bed early with a headache on the day the Locks left for London. Her sister kept her company and they had only just changed into their night things when they were startled by a violent ringing at the door.

'We listened – & heard the voice of M: d'Arblay – & Jerry [the servant] answering "They've gone to Bed." – "*Comment?* – What?"

cried he, – "*C'est impossible!* Vhat you say?" – Jerry then, to show his new education in this new Colony, said "*Allée couchée!*" It rained furiously – & we were quite grieved – but there was no help. He left a book for M*ᶩᶩᵉ* Burnet, & word that Mad*ᵉ* de Staël *could not* come on account of the bad weather. M*ʳ* Ferdinand [Narbonne's private secretary who had followed him to England] was with him, & has bewailed the disaster; and M. Siccard says he accompanied them till he was quite wet through his *redingotte* – but this enchanting M. d'Arblay will murmur at nothing.'

The whole party called again next day 'just as we had dined, for a morning visit'. (Mrs Phillips would have dined at two or three, the Juniperians at the fashionably later hour of five.) Madame de Staël was eager to share in d'Arblay's English lessons. She had learnt the language as a child; intellectually force-fed by her mother, her first English textbook was *Paradise Lost*. She referred to it in her first English note to Fanny Burney:

'When I first learned to read english I began by milton to know or renounce all at once. I follow the same system in writing my first english letter to miss burney; after such an enterprize nothing can affright me. I feel for her so tender a friendship that it melts my admiration, inspires my heart with hope of her indulgence and impresses me with the idea that in a tongue even unknown I could express sentiments so deeply felt.

'my servant returns for a french answer. I intreat miss burney to correct the words but preserve the sense.

'best compliments to my dear protectress, Madame Philippe.'

It was a note 'quite beautiful in ideas, and not very reprehensible in idiom', thought Fanny.

And here, with further graceful compliments, is a theme from Narbonne:

'As it is more easy for me to find words than ideas, and certainly as I have nothing better to do than to improve my memery in a society where every remembrance is so delightful, I have a desire to tell you a story. M*ᵉ* de Grafigni, author of the Peruvian letters, one of the best novels in our linguage was, like a certain English lady adored at Juniper, the most feeling and the best natured woman upon earth, but almost contrary to our English angel, she was not the most pleasing and the most amiable. Being asked once why, writing so perfectly well, she spoke sometimes so commonly, the reason is, said she, that I speak just what I am erasing. I don't know if the author of Cecilia ever wanted to erase anything. If she has, I entreat her to give me her erasings, and I am sure that I shall be the most clever fellow in the three kingdoms.'

Fanny could seldom remember spending her time so pleasantly. Her sister's children were delightful; Captain Phillips, often brusque and overbearing, was out of the way; above all, there were daily visits to Juniper Hall. The daytime was passed 'in scholaring', most often with d'Arblay, less frequently with Madame de Staël and Narbonne, the most fluent English-speaker of the group. Narbonne, she noted, showed signs of coming round to her views on the dangers of reform:

'The dread consequences & successful villainies which have followed the Revolution, & the murder of the innocent King, seem more and more deeply to affect him. Mad^e de Staël absolutely accuses him of *aristocracy* & says she is sure *I* commend his English more than her's from such sympathy. – I told her I should be proud of such a cause of partiality. We are very good friends, you will imagine, by my daring at such *waggery*.'

The evenings were given up to conversation and sometimes to reading aloud. Madame de Staël read extracts from her essay on the passions, which d'Arblay was engaged in transcribing, and blinded them all, wrote Fanny, with her reading of Voltaire's tragedy *Tancrède*. Fanny was too bashful to speak French in company – unlike her sister she had never been to France – still less to agree to Madame de Staël's persuasions that she should read Shakespeare in return. But she listened, bright-eyed and demure, to the ebb and flow of conversation, the elegant Narbonne, the deep-voiced Talleyrand, 'terse and *fin*', the ingenuous d'Arblay and, animating all with the zest of 'wit, deep thinking and light speaking', the ambassadress herself. 'Ah what days were those of conversational perfection,' sighed Fanny later, 'of wit, gaiety, repartee, information, badinage and eloquence.'

'Tell, my dear,' wrote Madame de Staël in another English note to Fanny Burney, 'if this day is a charming one, if it must be a sweet epoch in my life? – do you come to dine here with your lovely sister, and do you stay night and day till our sad separation. I rejoice me with that hope during this week; do not deceive my heart.

'I hope that card very clear, *mais, pour plus de certitude, je vous dis en français que votre chambre, la maison, les habitants de Juniper, tout est prêt à reçevoir la première femme de l'Angleterre.*'

From almost the day of their first meeting, Madame de Staël had been pressing Fanny Burney to come and stay at Juniper Hall. Now, with Fanny's Surrey visit coming to an end, she begged her to extend her stay by spending a 'large week' with her before returning home to Dr Burney. Fanny was tempted; d'Arblay's presence was a further unspoken attraction.

'I find her impossible to resist,' she told her father, '& therefore if your answer is as I conclude it must be, I shall wait upon her for a week.'

But Fanny Burney and her sister, in the rural seclusion of Surrey, knew nothing of the rumours that were circulating about Madame de Staël and her friends in London. Madame de Staël's liaison with Narbonne had been common knowledge – and the subject of scurrilous satires in the press – in France; it was bound to be discussed by the royalist émigrés and their friends in Tory circles. Some hints of what they were saying had reached the ears of Dr Burney. His first thought was for his daughter's reputation. Unmarried and dependent on royal approval for her pension, her position was especially delicate.

'I am not at all surprised,' he wrote, 'at your acc^t of the captivating powers of Mad^e de Stahl. It corresponds with all I had heard ab^t her & with the opinion I formed of her intellectual & literary powers on reading her charming little "Apologie de Rousseau". – But as nothing human is allowed to be perfect, she has not escaped censure. Her house was the centre of Revolutionists previous to the 10 Augt after her Father's departure, & she has been accused of partiality to M. de Narbonne. – But perhaps all may be Jacobinical Malignity. However unfavourable stories of her have been brought hither – & the Burkes & Mrs Ord have repeated them to me.'

She must remember, he continued, that amongst the royalist émigrés in London the constitutionalists were regarded with even greater horror than the actual government in France. If she were not already actually installed with Madame de Staël it might be possible to waive the visit, on the excuse of doing something for her sister, and spend the extra week with her instead.

Fanny Burney was shocked by her father's letter. Madame de Staël's house had not been a centre for the revolutionists, she told him, but for the constitutionalists who at that time were not only members of the government but firm supporters of the King. 'The Aristocrates were then already banished, or wanderers from fear, or concealed & silent from cowardice: & the Jacobins – – – I need not, after what I have already related, mention how utterly abhorrent to her must be that fiend-like set.'

As for the suggestion about Narbonne, she regarded it as a gross calumny:

'She loves him even tenderly, but so openly, so simply, so unaffectedly, & with such utter freedom from all coquetry, that if they were two Men, or two women, the affection could not, I think, be more obviously undesigning. She is very plain; – he is very handsome; – her intellectual endowments must be with him her sole attraction. M. de Talleyrand was another of her society [in Paris], & she seems equally attached to him. M. le Duc [sic] de Montmorenci, she loves, she says, as her Brother, he is another of this bright constellation . . . In short her whole coterie live together as Brethren . . . Indeed I think you could not spend a Day with them and not see that their commerce is that of pure, but exalted & most elegant, Friendship.'

The sharp-eyed Fanny, so quick to notice and record the frailties of her fellow-countrymen, was singularly naïve when it came to other nationalities. But though she indignantly defended her new friends, she shared her father's fear of scandal. 'I would give the world . . . to avoid being a GUEST under their roof, now I have heard even a shadow of such a rumour,' she wrote, '– & I *will*, if it be *possible* without hurting or offending them.' She had already refused the invitation to stay at Juniper Hall, though Madame de Staël – not surprisingly – had seemed bewildered by her excuses. But her sister and Captain Phillips were intending to go to London the following week and she planned to return on the same day. Any embarrassments therefore would not be for long.

She finished her letter with further details of her friends.

D'Arblay, she wrote, had been commander of the frontier town of Longwy, and though he had left it to serve with Lafayette before its fall to the Prussians, he had written to the National Convention to refute the charges that the King had done nothing to defend it, enclosing a letter from Dumouriez, then Minister of War, commending the efforts that had been made there. Malesherbes had hoped to use the letter in the King's defence, but for fear perhaps of antagonizing Dumouriez, had not been able to do so.

'M. d'Arblay,' she continued, 'in quitting France, with La Fayette, upon the deposition of the King, had only some ready money in his pocket – & he has been *décreté* since, & all he was worth in the World is sold and seized by the Convention! – M. de Narbonne loves him as the tenderest of Brothers, & while *one* has a Guinea in the World, the *other* will have half. "Ah!" cried M. d'Arblay upon the murder of the King, which almost annihilated him, "I know not how those can *exist* who have any feelings of *Remorse* when *I* scarce can endure my life from the simple feeling of *regret* that ever I pronounced the word LIBERTY – IN FRANCE!"'

Chapter 6

———————————— ⌒ ————————————

Three days after the execution of Louis XVI, Chauvelin, the acting French ambassador, was expelled from London. For the first three years of the Revolution Britain had maintained a policy of strict neutrality towards France. But the French invasion of Belgium, their opening of the river Scheldt to commerce in defiance of treaties, the threat to Britain's vital interests in Holland which the French army was poised to invade, had brought the two countries to the brink of war. The death of the King was no more than a final provocation. 'To the Kings of Europe,' roared Danton in the National Convention, 'we throw down as a gage of battle, the head of a King.' On 31 January, pre-empting the British government, France declared war on Britain and Holland. It was the start of a conflict that would last for more than twenty years.

In the war fever which swept the country, it was natural that the French in Britain, above all the constitutionalists, should be regarded with increased suspicion. With the Aliens bill like a sword of Damocles above their heads, it seemed more and more advisable for the Juniper Hall colony to keep a low profile and wait quietly on events.

Madame de Staël, in theory at least, was well aware of the need to avoid being noticed. 'I'm stifling with good behaviour,' she wrote to

Gibbon. But hers was not a light which could easily be hid under a bushel. The political hatreds she and her friends aroused, the gossip which linked her name to Narbonne's, soon came more forcibly to Dr Burney, with a warning letter from a family friend, James Hutton.

'It is talked,' he wrote, 'that Mad. de Staël Necker's Daughter boasts of an intimacy with my dear Fanny Burney as if they were often and much together, now Madame de Staël has Infamy on her Head as an intriguing woman, not only is she Diabolical Democrate, but came to England to intrigue here, and to follow Mr de Narbonne this being generally talked, I do not wish our Fanny to have the slightest Connection with such an Adulterous Demoniac . . . Fanny's Celebrity is just, no wonder if she is sought so by Foreigners now Mad. de Staël may well wish for her advantage, what would be most Horrible Prejudicial to Fanny.'

'Good God, my dearest Father, what a dreadful letter is this of Mr Hutton's!' wrote Fanny on receiving it; '– it is impossible to me or to Susan, seeing all we see, to credit what we hear.' It had given her a sleepless night, she told him, and by the same post had come a letter from Mrs Lock still further sounding the alarm. Unlike Mr Hutton, Mrs Lock had refused to accept the rumours which were circulating, though such was the atmosphere in London that it was difficult to refute them effectively. One might as well try to defend Guy Fawkes as Talleyrand, she wrote, and things were little better where Madame de Staël was concerned. Liberal and generous-minded, she had no intention of letting such rumours affect her friendship for the Juniperians. Susanna Phillips felt the same, though she saw the problems involved. 'I am persuaded that Madame de Staël is calumniated in her private character as she has been in her political principles,' she wrote, 'but unfortunately she is so little governed by the common rules, even those of France, that I am aware of the extreme difficulty there would be in attempting to vindicate her.'

Fanny Burney had more to lose. Her pension depended on the approval of the royal family; even the suggestion of an unsuitable friendship could do her harm. The upper reaches of the aristocracy, the Devonshire House set, the circle round the Prince of Wales, could allow themselves as free a life as their equivalents in France. But such liberty, even had she wished it, was not available to Fanny.

With no advantages of wealth and birth, her acceptance in society, above all in the stuffy atmosphere of Court, depended on an unblemished reputation. She staunchly defended the ambassadress in a letter to James Hutton – she knew he had friends in Court circles and would pass the letter on. But she determined to run no risk of visiting Juniper Hall again.

Fortunately a sore throat of the 'putrid sort' came to her aid and she was able to use it as her excuse to avoid all further invitations. On 26 February, her sore throat recovered, she returned to London and her father's apartments at Chelsea College, where he had been the official organist for the last ten years. She had not seen Madame de Staël again, but d'Arblay had come to say goodbye and to beg his 'dear master in gown', as he called her, to continue their exchange of themes. Fanny, surprised and touched, agreed and at the same time, imploring his discretion, was able to hint at the reasons which had kept her from Juniper Hall.

Back in London, she found that Mr Hutton and Mrs Lock had not exaggerated the way that tongues were wagging. Her first themes to d'Arblay returned to the distressing subject. It gave her the greatest pain to say so, she told him – she felt for Madame de Staël with all her heart. But such was the feeling against her that her presence in England did more harm to Narbonne's reputation than even his worst enemies could have done. To her father and stepmother she had talked so much of Madame de Staël's good and noble qualities that she had almost succeeded in converting them. But to the world in general such arguments had proved useless. 'She is neither banished nor an émigrée,' was the cry, 'it is M. de Narbonne who has seduced her from her husband and her children.' In vain she talked of the different manners and customs in France. 'She is a wife, she is a mother,' was the only response.

D'Arblay, devoted to Narbonne, felt bound to warn him of the scandal that was brewing, though he realized sadly that Madame de Staël, 'unjustly judged in this fortunate country', might be driven to return to Switzerland and would do her best to get Narbonne to follow. Meanwhile, abandoning the vehicle of their themes – Fanny had written to him in French – he returned to his own language to write a defence of Madame de Staël.

46

'What have people been saying to you about Madame de Staël?' he wrote. 'They wrong her if they do not do justice to her eminent qualities of heart and mind. Her kindness, her humanity, her benevolence and the need she has to exercise it, are unequalled.'

It might well be that ill-natured stories had been spread about her – he had no wish to ask for further details. But her faults, if they existed, were as nothing to her talents and her even greater virtues. Madame de Staël had been moved to tears by the domestic happiness of families such as the Locks. But in France, above all in the highest circles, the marriage bond was regarded very differently. All women, more or less, were victims of marriages of convenience. It would be barbarous to judge them by the standards that applied in England. In any case, whatever their previous relations might have been, he could swear on his honour that Madame de Staël was living now on terms of purest friendship with Narbonne. He would recommend his sister or his mother to her company.

D'Arblay was obviously sincere in what he wrote to Fanny Burney. Gradually, tentatively, their correspondence had grown deeper and more personal; he had a sensibility that matched her own, an openness and sincerity that shone through all he wrote. But he had probably misjudged the situation between Madame de Staël and Narbonne. At the time of Narbonne's escape from Paris, her letters tell us, she had made a vow that if he was spared her relationship with him would be pure from then on. At some time or other in England, as later letters make clear, her resolution foundered. Madame de Staël never found it easy to say no, perhaps, as an unkind contemporary suggested, because being uncertain of her physical attractions she was always glad of reassurance.

At one point, however, d'Arblay was touching on a central problem in Madame de Staël's life. Time and again she returned in her writings to the theme of an unhappy marriage, to the joy that a woman could find were she only matched to a husband who was worthy of her. Baron de Staël had married her blatantly for her money; any hopes she had brought to her marriage had been quickly dissipated. 'He is a perfectly decent man,' she wrote, 'incapable of doing or saying a stupid thing, but sterile and without resources; he cannot make me unhappy because he can contribute nothing to my happiness.' In her relations with other men she seemed doomed to constant disillusion. She had hoped at one point she might divorce Staël for Narbonne; her lover's lack of enthusiasm and the financial problems involved had soon dispelled the idea. But all her life, in the absence of a satisfactory husband, she sought for a man to whom she could devote herself. The very intensity of her pursuit drove those she sought away.

To outsiders such as Mrs Phillips, unaware of any deeper issues, it was plain that Narbonne was often embarrassed by Madame de Staël. 'Their minds in some points ought to be exchanged,' she wrote, 'for he is as delicate as a really feminine woman and evidently suffers when he sees her setting *les bienséances* aside, as it often enough falls to her to do.'

There were obvious tensions in their present situation. Perhaps because of this Madame de Staël had started writing to her husband in the hope of getting him to England and thereby refuting the rumours which were going round. Staël proved unresponsive; he had his own problems as an ambassador, out of favour with the Swedish Court and in danger of losing his post altogether. The political intrigues of his wife in the period up to 10 August had done him no good in the eyes of his superiors. Unrepentant, Madame de Staël continued to pull out every stop in demanding his presence or at the very least his company in escorting her back across war-torn Europe to Switzerland, where she hoped Narbonne would follow her.

In the meantime, despite the uncertainties of the future, there were still the pleasures of company and conversation and, with the approach of spring, the charms of rural life to savour. Susanna Phillips wrote delightedly of picking violets with her children in the woods below Norbury Park, 'the white house appearing like a Temple of Fame'. Madame de Staël, so much a romantic in other respects, had no time for the romantic attitude to nature. The scenery of Switzerland left her cold; confronted with the view of Lake Geneva she sighed for Paris and 'the gutter of the rue du Bac'. But her lover's presence lent enchantment to the Surrey landscape and she would look back with nostalgia to the woods round Juniper Hall and the rolling views from Norbury Park. The warmer weather tempted her to expeditions in the neighbourhood, sometimes on foot, sometimes in the shabby cabriolet which one or other of her friends took turns to drive. There were seats for only two in front but there was a dickey for a servant at the back; the communicating glass between had been broken so that whoever rode behind should not be left out of the conversation. As she bowled along the narrow lanes, with Narbonne and Talleyrand as her companions, she declared that she had never heard more brilliant talk.

Talleyrand, at first a privileged exile, since he at least had left Paris with a passport, was now no better off than Narbonne and those other liberal aristocrats who had been forced to leave the country after 10 August. On 20 November a safe containing papers – the famous iron chest – had been discovered in the King's apartments in the Tuileries. Amongst the compromising papers it contained were two letters in which Talleyrand was mentioned as someone who would be prepared to serve the King. It had been enough to brand him as a traitor in the National Convention's eyes. Despite his protests, his name was placed on the list of proscribed émigrés and his property was automatically forfeit to the state.

For Talleyrand, as for Narbonne, Madame de Staël was an ever-generous friend. But her own position was precarious. Not only was her father's property at risk in France, thanks to his ill-timed defence of the King, but her mother, increasingly unhappy at the scandal of her absence, was goading him to withdraw all further remittances if she did not return. Fears about money overshadowed the spirits of all the Juniper Hall party, though it would have been considered tedious to dwell upon them. 'I have always noticed,' wrote a great lady of the time, 'that it is a sign of low birth and a low mind to complain of deprivation except very casually.'

Fanny Burney was well aware of the colony's difficulties. Narbonne, she knew, had hopes of obtaining funds from Saint Domingue in the West Indies, where his wife owned an estate and where the colonists were in rebellion against the National Convention; meanwhile he had the residue of some £4000 with which he had arrived in England but which, little realizing how long his exile might be, he had run through all too quickly. ('Narbonne, as I have come to know him,' noted Bollman in a letter to his family, 'is extremely extravagant and spendthrift to the point of profligacy.') Talleyrand was not altogether without resources – he had taken the precaution of transferring his valuable library to England during his diplomatic mission there the previous summer, and was planning to sell it in London. D'Arblay, who had left France with nothing but his baggage and a little ready money, was the worst off of them all. It was to him that Fanny Burney's heart went out. A few weeks after her return to London, emboldened by the growing sympathy between them, she wrote him a letter in which with great delicacy she offered him a loan. By a chance she had no time to explain, she told him, she happened to have £100 at her disposal which she could lend without interest to whomever she wished. If ever – unhappily – so trivial a sum could be of use to him she begged him to let her be his first banker. He had promised her to read the letter in the spirit she had written it, as though it were a sister's to a brother.

The letter was written in French, for they were still continuing their exchange of themes. It was annotated and dated later in Fanny Burney's hand: '30 March, 1793. This – by its *consequences* proved at once the last of my *Thèmes* – & the first of my *Letters* – to Him who became in Four Months, my best of Friends, my honoured Husband – '.

Chapter 7

Madame de Staël had been puzzled and a little hurt by Fanny Burney's refusal to stay with her at Juniper Hall. From d'Arblay's tactful hints she had gathered something of the political hostility towards her in London and of the rumours concerning her relationship with Narbonne. But she was unaware of their full extent. In London Fanny Burney, alarmed by the way her name was being linked with Madame de Staël's, had sought an audience with the Queen in which she had virtually promised to break off all relations with her. 'You did well to forsake such devilisms,' wrote Mr Hutton approvingly, ' . . . I trust I was not capable for a moment of supposing that she [the Queen] would not do your Truth the justice it deserves.'

In dissociating herself from Madame de Staël Fanny Burney was influenced by prudery and caution, but perhaps still more by the fact that her friendship with d'Arblay would be less open to criticism if she did so. It was bad enough – in Tory eyes – that he was a constitutionalist. But by differentiating between him and public figures like Madame de Staël, Narbonne and Talleyrand, she could draw their fire to some extent. Her prudent policy was thrown into confusion, however, when towards the middle of March an affectionate letter arrived from Madame de Staël. She was planning a visit to

London the following week and hoped to call on Miss Burney at Chelsea College. Sublimely unaware of Fanny's feelings, she thanked her for the good will she had shown in the midst of the attacks against her.

'They'll tell you I'm a democrat,' she wrote, 'and they forget that my friends and I have escaped the daggers of the Jacobins; they'll say I love to meddle in politics and yet here I am at a time when M. de Staël is begging me to go to Paris where he's involved in affairs of the utmost importance . . . Finally they go so far as to trouble the repose of friendship, refusing to accept that whilst remaining faithful to my duties I felt the need to share for two months in the unhappiness of the man whose life I had saved.'

Fanny awaited her arrival with misgiving. Her father, disturbed by Mr Hutton's warnings, and firmly Tory in his outlook, already disapproved of her friendship with the constitutionalists. Her difficult stepmother (christened La Dama by her stepchildren) was still more steeped in prejudice and could be relied upon to make things unpleasant. All Fanny could hope for was that the visit would go off discreetly, and encounters with her parents be avoided.

In the event she was out when Madame de Staël arrived, but the ambassadress was undeterred. 'Nothing could happen more perversely than the events of this day,' wrote Fanny to Susanna Phillips that evening. 'Poor M^e de S[taël] was *let in* and boasts she had a most courteous reception from La Dama with whom she spent quarter of an hour!' To make matters worse, her old friend Mrs Ord, an arch-Tory and arch-gossip, had called at the house while Madame de Staël was there. Redirected to Sloane Street where Fanny was spending the day with another sister, Charlotte Francis, she arrived there some time later to find that Madame de Staël had once again preceded her. Ostentatiously withdrawing herself from such company, she refused to come in and though Fanny rushed down in an effort to appease her, she had driven off in disapproval, leaving Madame de Staël in possession of the field.

'It was an infinitely indiscreet kindness in this poor ardent woman who was so charming, so open, so delightful herself that, while she was with me I forgot all the mischiefs that might follow,' continued Fanny. 'To add to all this comes another Letter from M. de

N[arbonne], offering to spend the day at Chelsea! How will all this be blazoned! – & how duped is the unsuspecting Character who fancies she has made a friend! – I am inexpressibly disturbed by the expectation of this event's spreading to the Q[ueen's] H[ouse] & occasioning fresh terrors . . . What in the World can I do – and to make all Vexations worse my good Master of the Language, who alone could come unblamed, only called & asked for you & then went out.'

Missing d'Arblay had been the crowning perversity of the day for Fanny Burney. But together with his friends he was spending a week in London, and she had the chance to see him several times when he was visiting the Locks. On the neutral ground of their drawing room in Portland Square even Madame de Staël and Talleyrand could be encountered with impunity. The conversation tended to be general, but on the last of these occasions, in a brief exchange with d'Arblay, Fanny caught a glimpse of the anxiety and misery his good manners normally concealed. She had written to him the next morning with her offer of a loan.

D'Arblay refused her offer. But this 'last of my *Thèmes* & the first of my *Letters*', as she called it, had touched him to the heart. 'I will not speak of gratitude,' he wrote, 'but I must tell you that nothing in my life has ever given me such pleasure as your offer, which had it come from anyone else, perhaps, would have humiliated and insulted me, however much I appreciated the generosity which lay behind it.'

He was writing in French for he had serious things to say. He had been spending the day, he told her, preparing a memorandum on raising a French troop of horse to be used in defending the British coast against invasion. On the strength of this memorandum, addressed to John Villiers, Member of Parliament for Dartmouth and an old acquaintance of Narbonne's, he hoped to be appointed agent for one of the emigrant French corps then being recruited in England. If his project proved successful, and in doing so he could earn enough to stay in England, there was one person – *une personne* – with whom he wished to share his fortunes. Without this person's approval his plan would have no further interest for him and he would abandon it entirely. 'Try to work out the meaning of this riddle,' he told her, 'and write to me as frankly as I have to you.'

D'Arblay's letter, timid and hedged with conditionals, was nothing less than a tentative proposal of marriage. Penniless, exiled, politically unwelcome, he knew how little he had to offer in worldly terms. Fanny had suspected something of his feelings while never thinking he would utter them. But her first thought on receiving his letter was not of his disadvantages but hers.

'O my dearest *dear* Susan! what would I not give to have you with me at this moment,' she wrote, enclosing d'Arblay's letter. 'You to whom alone I could open my heart – labouring at this instant with feelings that almost burst it . . . I will be quite – quite open – & tell you that everything upon Earth I could ever covet for the peculiar happiness of my peculiar mind seems here united – were there not one scruple in the way . . . Can you not guess what it is? – I wish him a *younger Partner*. I do not wish myself richer – grander – more powerful or higher born – one of his first attractions with me is his superiority to all such considerations – no I wish myself only to be *younger*.'

'*Your* scruple I never could have devined,' wrote Mrs Phillips in reply. D'Arblay was thirty-nine and looked more; from everything she had seen and judged of him, Fanny would be no more dear to him if she were ten years younger. 'But – but – but – You do not wish yourself *richer* you say! Ah my Fanny! – but that would be essentially requisite in such a union – your single £100 per ann. – and his – Alas! his NOTHING – How would it be possible for you then to live?'

Here was the nub of the problem. And Fanny's pension, small as it was, was dependent on the Queen's approval. As a Frenchman and a constitutionalist, d'Arblay would be doubly suspect. His hopes of employment as an agent she knew to be far-fetched. Conscious of the difficulties ahead, Fanny could give no immediate answer. But reassured as to her 'one scruple', she could not bear to leave him altogether in suspense. In a brief note of reply enclosed in a letter to her sister – she dared not let her writing be seen at Juniper Hall for fear of irritating Madame de Staël – she made it clear that her feelings, at least, were not in doubt. If his plans to stay in England depended on her, she wrote, she did not think that he would leave the country.

While Fanny Burney and d'Arblay were indirectly declaring their love for one another, Madame de Staël had been filling her brief stay in London with a whirlwind of activity. If some Tory doors were closed to her, she had enough introductions in grand London circles from Gibbon and her father to ensure that her days and nights were full. At an evening with Gibbon's friend Lord Sheffield, we see her in conversation with the newly-appointed Lord Chancellor, Lord Loughborough. Accustomed as he was to the more reserved behaviour of his countrywomen, the Chancellor was astonished, and not best pleased, to be plunged into a far-ranging discussion of politics and the principles of government. 'There's a lot of bad feeling against her here,' Sheffield confided to Gibbon. 'She's made out to be the worst type of intriguing democrat, capable of setting the Thames on fire. I've had the greatest trouble convincing people that she's eminently lively, agreeable and blessed with extraordinary intellectual gifts, though at times she can seem ridiculous.'

In the more impoverished company of the exiled constitutionalists, Madame de Staël renewed old acquaintances at parties where the sparkle of the conversation made up for the sparseness of the fare. London was crowded with refugees from France, most of them living on the brink of poverty, reduced to menial occupations to survive, the women embroidering or laundering, or making the chip straw hats that were the fashion of the day, the men teaching French or fencing, or even, in the case of one accomplished émigré, playing second fiddle in an orchestra. 'I promise not to look surprised,' whispered Talleyrand to his old friend Madame de Genlis, when, thanks to an unexpected windfall, she managed for once to give her guests a decent meal.

With Talleyrand in attendance the ambassadress was guest of honour of the Comtesse de Flahaut, Talleyrand's former mistress. Having tired of making the inevitable straw hats, she was writing a novel, *Adèle de Senange,* to augment her income; Talleyrand obligingly offered to correct her proofs. In her 'miserable lodging above a grocer's' the conversation lasted till two in the morning with Madame de Staël, not unwilling to outshine a former rival, at her most eloquent and brilliant.

Refreshed by her sortie to London but conscious of the dangers of over-exposure, Madame de Staël returned to Juniper Hall towards the end of March. D'Arblay followed her there a few days later. Mrs Phillips's first thoughts were of him and her sister and she anxiously

55

followed each new development of their romance. 'Ah my Fanny! Were there ever times as interesting as the present?' she sighed. But she was swept up as well in the life of Juniper Hall and with a pen as lively as her sister's she once more caught their gatherings on the wing.

On 1 April, for instance, impelled by an 'irresistible invitation to dine', she attended a reading of Lally Tollendal's famous tragedy, *La Mort de Strafford*. A noted orator, who had been called 'the Cicero of France', Lally Tollendal was sadly disappointing in the flesh – 'large, fat, with a great head, small nose, immense cheeks . . . *un très honnête garçon* as M. de Talleyrand says of him *et rien de plus*' – while his tragedy and the 'alternate howling and thundering of his voice in declaiming' left her more inclined to laugh than cry. D'Arblay, who had arrived half way through dinner, had slipped away to his room immediately after. He was sent for several times after coffee in order that the reading might begin, and Madame de Staël at last impatiently proposed beginning without him. '"*Mais cela lui fera de la peine*," said M. d'Autun [Talleyrand] good naturedly; and as she persisted he rose up and limped out of the room to fetch him; he succeeded in bringing him.' Perhaps he was determined his friend should not escape.

Lally Tollendal and the Princesse d'Hénin, a *faux ménage* long sanctified by time, left next morning. Relieved of the playwright's ponderous presence, the evening saw the party in a lighter mood.

'Madame de Staël was very gay and M. de Talleyrand very *comique* this evening,' wrote Mrs Phillips, once again a welcome guest. They talked over friends and acquaintances 'with the utmost unreserve and sometimes with the most comic humour imaginable', while Talleyrand teased Madame de Staël. 'He criticized amongst other things her reading of prose with great *sangfroid*: "You read prose very badly; you have a sing song way of reading which won't do at all; listening to you one thinks one is hearing poetry and this makes a very bad impression."'

D'Arblay's manner had been quiet and thoughtful during these last few days; he spent long hours in his room completing his memorandum for Villiers. But that evening Mrs Phillips was able to hand him the note in which Fanny Burney, without committing herself entirely, gave him her much desired response. D'Arblay was unable to conceal his joy. He kissed Mrs Phillips's hand repeatedly as he handed her into the carriage to drive her to Juniper Hall, tying her cloak and bonnet lovingly round her and forbidding her to speak on the drive lest the cold night air should make her cough. At dinner he was 'gay, entertaining, charming'. 'I don't know when I have seen him in such a flow of spirits,' wrote Susanna, 'certainly not when Madame de Staël is present.'

The following day, leaving early in the morning, he disappeared from Juniper Hall, to the mystification of Narbonne, who told Mrs Phillips he had no idea where he had gone. He returned on horseback late that afternoon and little Norbury, Mrs Phillips's eight-year-old son, heard him tell Narbonne that he had walked eighteen or twenty miles of the way to London but had not seen the person he had hoped to see.

Dining with the Phillipses that evening – d'Arblay had been too tired to join them – Madame de Staël was '*toute émerveillée*' at his expedition and insisted that Mrs Phillips should tell her where he had been if he told her.

'But he'll tell Mrs Phillips in confidence,' said Narbonne, 'for he prides himself a little on her kindness and goodwill.'

'*C'est égal*,' said Madame de Staël, 'you can perfectly well repeat it to me afterwards.'

Narbonne and the ambassadress had been mystified by d'Arblay's errand. Fanny Burney, at Chelsea College, could have given them the answer. She had spent the morning on a round of calls but had been so agitated by her private preoccupations that even a visit to her 'dearest Mrs Lock' had given her no pleasure. That afternoon she was sitting with her father in his study when Molly, the servant girl, came in with a rose tree and a letter which had been left, she said, by someone who did not wish to wait. Knowing it to be Cart Day – the day when a provision cart came up from Norbury Park to London – she immediately assumed that the rose tree was a present from the Locks till she saw that the accompanying letter was from d'Arblay.

'My Father immediately asked if it was in Mrs Lock's Hand – I concluded all now would follow! – & I felt almost ready to die – I was

57

forced to answer – "No – Sir – 'tis a Thème – I believe – from M. d'Arblay – I suppose they both came by the Cart . . . "

'My ever unsuspicious Father, with his usual sweetness, asked nothing more, & was perfectly content. Having occasionally read him some parts of some of the Themes, he hears of them as matters of course, without surmise or curiosity. How fortunate La Dama was not present!'

The rose tree was a gift from d'Arblay who had come up to London specially to see her but, hearing she was not alone, had preferred not to speak to her in the midst of her family. In his letter he described his continuing hopes of finding employment in England.

'My ambitions are not great,' he told Fanny, 'and if I were able, without appearing too ridiculous, to speak openly of what I have hitherto only dared mention in veiled terms – I should be the happiest man in the world.'

'Ah, my dearest Susanna,' wrote Fanny, ' . . . Were he secure of only Bread & Water, I am *very* sure I should gaily partake of them with him.' But with so many worldly obstacles to overcome before she could be sure of her pension at least, she dared not show her full feelings as yet. She must give him confidence in her 'faithful – but not *fervant* regard' while she reflected on the tricky path she had to follow. D'Arblay, spontaneous, open, unaware of the pitfalls of English Court life, could not help her there. Her answer once more stalled for time, but there was a gaiety and lightness in its tone that told its own story. She was deeply touched by his journey, she hoped very much that his memorandum would be successful, and she thanked him for the rose tree, so pretty, so elegant and so sweet that she had done nothing but admire it since.

Chapter 8

Amongst the visitors to Juniper Hall in the spring of 1793 was the young Dr Bollman, who had stayed on in London, taking lodgings in Ludgate Hill, after Narbonne left for Surrey. He had gained a certain reputation from his rescue of Narbonne; he would later be involved, unsuccessfully, in planning Lafayette's escape from his prison in the Austrian fortress of Olmutz. However, despite his first enthusiastic admiration, he had fallen out with Narbonne who, effusive though his thanks had been, had seemed to Bollman to be condescending. He had touchily refused the offer of a pension from Narbonne who, somewhat optimistically, considering his own ruined state, had promised to pay him £50 a year. But Madame de Staël on her visit to London had succeeded in soothing his susceptibilities. 'We are all good children,' she told him in his native German, 'and must not quarrel.' She invited him to Surrey, making much of him, he wrote with satisfaction to his family, playing him sweet airs on the piano and singing Italian songs. He was amazed by her constant activity.

'This Staël is a genius,' he wrote, 'an extraordinary eccentric woman in everything she says or does. She sleeps only a few hours and for the rest of the time she is uninterruptedly and fearfully busy . . . Whilst her hair is being done, while she breakfasts, in fact

59

for a third of the day, she writes. She has not sufficient quiet to look over what she has written, but even the rough outpourings of her ever active mind are of the greatest interest.'

Often out of his depth in the general conversation but proud too of his moral independence, Bollman observed his fellow guests, Narbonne and Talleyrand in particular, with a perceptive eye.

'Narbonne is rather a big man,' he wrote, 'a bit heavy but vigorous, with something striking and superior about his features. He has an inexhaustible supply of wit and ideas and possesses all the social graces to the highest degree . . . when he wishes too he can attract irresistibly, and even intoxicate, a single person or a roomful of people.'

There was only one person in France to be compared with him in this respect, who in Bollman's opinion far surpassed him, his friend the former bishop of Autun:

'Narbonne pleases but tires one in the end: one could on the contrary listen to Talleyrand for ever. Narbonne seeks to please and one feels it; Talleyrand speaks without the slightest effort and seems to exist in an atmosphere of perfect calm and relaxation. Narbonne's conversation is more brilliant; Talleyrand's is more graceful, more subtle, more incisive. Narbonne is not the man for every one; sentimental people can't bear him and he has no hold over them. But Talleyrand, while no less morally corrupt, can move to tears even those who despise him.'

With such dangerously fascinating company to choose from it was hardly surprising that Madame de Staël found her English neighbours disappointing. She made an exception for the Locks and one or two others: Mr Benn, a nabob, 'immensely rich', the Talbots of nearby Mickleham Park. But the majority of local gentry with their talk of hunting and their stiflingly domesticated wives were hard to swallow. In her novel *Corinne* the ardent and creative heroine (an idealized self-portrait) is condemned to a spell of English country life, her talents discounted, any spark of feeling or originality regarded as ill-bred. An after-dinner conversation where the ladies await their husbands who are lingering over their port has the ring of unhappy experience:

'"My dear," said one lady to another, "do you think the water has been boiling long enough to make the tea?" "My dear," replied the other, "I think it's a little too early; the gentlemen won't be ready yet." "Do you think they'll stay long at table today?" asked a third. "I really couldn't say," replied a fourth, "they may spend a while discussing the next week's elections." "No, no, my dear," says a fifth, "they're probably talking over last week's hunting which starts again on Monday; they should be finished pretty soon." "Ah, I hardly think so," sighed a sixth, and silence fell once more.'

It was not to be expected that Madame de Staël would put up with this kind of thing. Her English neighbours, on the other hand, looked askance at her and her friends. Tories almost to a man, they feared the contagion of democratic French ideas; rumours of Madame de Staël's irregular amours had also begun to filter through from London. Mr Jenkinson, the landlord, a wealthy retired businessman who had built himself a new house higher up the hill – Juniper Hall, from its position in a valley, was locally known as Juniper Hole – showed signs of having second thoughts about his tenants. To allay his moral scruples he demanded an increase in the rent. Mrs Phillips, arriving unexpectedly one afternoon, found the Juniper Hall party in heated discussion with their landlord who had arrived with his attorney, an 'ill-looking personage', she wrote, who might have been drawn by Hogarth. Mr Clarke, the tutor, was spokesman for the party while Madame de Staël, in an effort to lighten the atmosphere, kept breaking in coquettishly, 'What will you, Mr Jenkinson? Tell to me what will you?' Narbonne, indignant at what he considered exorbitant demands, was far less gentle with him, and succeeded in reducing them considerably.

In the midst of these domestic pinpricks the Juniper Hall colony had been following events across the Channel with passionate attention. Whilst Britain's role had so far been confined to subsidizing Austria and Prussia and attacking French colonial possessions, her allies had succeeded in reversing France's triumphs of the autumn. On 16 March General Dumouriez, the hero of Valmy and Jemappes, was decisively defeated at Neerwinden in Holland. In Paris the Jacobins were gaining the ascendancy, using the mob to press their advantage over the more moderate Girondins. Dumouriez, a Girondin appointment, had already incurred the enmity of the

Jacobins by his protests at their violent policies. Aware that his defeat would probably cost him his life, he staked his future on a bold throw. Arresting the commissioners sent from Paris to dismiss him, he handed them over as hostages to the Austrians and on 1 April announced his intention of marching to Paris to restore order and thereafter negotiate for peace. 'It is time,' he declared, 'that the army fulfils its duty in purging France of agitators and assassins. It is time to return to a constitution.'

At the first hint of the news from France Talleyrand had returned to London. On 8 April, arriving hotfoot from the capital, he was able to communicate all he knew to the eager audience at Juniper Hall. 'Madame de Staël,' wrote Mrs Phillips, 'in a state of the most vehement impatience for news, would scarce give him time to breathe between her questions: and when she had heard all he could tell her, she was equally impetuous to hear his conjectures.' Talleyrand, though never losing his air of placid composure, was equally excited. Only Narbonne, grave and thoughtful, refused to join them in their speculations. To Madame de Staël's half-playful reproaches he replied that the events of the previous six months had shown him the futility of making any plans. 'However,' he added, 'in eight days from now it may be possible to judge more clearly and then – I will play my part.'

He said no more and fell into a reverie while Talleyrand continued to speculate on what the future held. There was no point in embarking on an ill-founded scheme, 'but I must admit,' he said laughingly, 'that I long to fight . . . it would give me the greatest pleasure to give a good beating to those disgusting wretches.'

'Ah, no,' said Narbonne gently and sadly, 'what possible pleasure can there be in killing pathetic creatures whose greatest crimes are ignorance and stupidity? If it were just a question of fighting Marat, Danton, Robespierre, M. Egalité* and a few hundred other such scoundrels I might perhaps find some satisfaction in it too.'

He sank back into his reverie, leaving the others to continue the conversation. Later that evening, as he drove Susanna Phillips

*Louis XVI's cousin, the Duc d'Orléans

home, he talked a little of the new turn of events, and Susanna, ever feeling, was able to tell him how much her thoughts were with him and his friends.

The proclamation of the Prince of Saxe Coburg, commander of the Austrian army, promising Dumouriez support whilst disclaiming any thought of conquest, gave a solider base to the colony's hopes. It was enough to bring them to London where Narbonne, with the eventual plan of joining Dumouriez, prepared a letter setting out the conditions – the restoration of the constitution and the monarchy – under which he would be prepared to support him. The letter was never sent, however, for scarcely had it been written than the news that Dumouriez, unable to rally the army to him, had defected to the Austrians put an end to all their hopes. It was a bitter disappointment, though Susanna and her sister found secret consolation in the thought of the dangers their friends had escaped.

D'Arblay, following Narbonne's initiative, had written to Dumouriez, recalling their comradeship in arms and promising him his support. Like Narbonne's, his letter was overtaken by events and it was never sent. Like Narbonne, too, he had come to London and Mrs Lock, in a letter to Susanna Phillips, described him as too agitated to join them for a supper party. 'Were politics, as she supposes, the sole cause of his agitation?' Susanna asked her sister coyly. Certainly, in the midst of so much public excitement and uncertainty, d'Arblay had not lost sight of his private concerns. Honour might possibly demand his return to France; his heart was already given in England. Chivalrous and high-minded, he brought to Fanny Burney a devotion as romantic in its way as that of her hero Lord Orville for her heroine Evelina. And as in her novel, the course of true love would be strewn with obstacles before it reached a happy ending.

At home, at Chelsea College, Fanny could not but be aware of the first and greatest drawback to her marriage with d'Arblay – his nationality. 'The more I think, the more I foresee of impediment – a clamour against a FRENCH man almost overwhelming,' she wrote to her sister. Only that afternoon the censorious Mrs Ord had been calling for the expulsion of all the French in England: in front of La Dama too, added Fanny, 'who, still more barbarously to Me, was pleased to *beg* in a whining tone of moderation, that the *Priests* might be exempt, though none other!'

The atmosphere of Chelsea College, which her stepmother's ill temper had always made uneasy, was unpropitious for lovers' meetings. But snatched moments of conversation, exchanged notes, shared glances, became perhaps the sweeter for their hostile background, and Fanny's courtship journals for her sister – a running narrative of the progress of her love affair – are as enchanting as anything she ever wrote. Her half-sister Sarah Harriet Burney, who later became a novelist herself, watched d'Arblay's visits with a knowing eye and made him a figure in her novel *Clarentine*. We see him there, a handsome French exile who 'found some pretext to come to the house almost every day. At one time it was with a book he had borrowed; at another with a note.' Other members of the household were less welcoming: the gossiping Swiss governess, consumed with spiteful curiosity, the stepmother who ostentatiously left the room whenever d'Arblay called.

'But why,' cried d'Arblay, half laughing, half affrighted, 'does Madame your mother always disappear?'

'I was fain to confess,' she wrote, 'that, *à la vérité*, she was sometimes a little Capricious.'

'O, as to that,' said d'Arblay coolly, 'I knew it already. Mrs Lock has told me all about it.'

A greater hurdle was her father's attitude. No one, in general, was more affable than Dr Burney. But his Tory prejudices, reinforced by the disastrous progress of the Revolution, were deeply engrained. D'Arblay, for all his personal misfortunes, remained an unrepentant liberal. Their first meeting was one of 'cold civility' on Dr Burney's part and the 'most agitated fervour' on d'Arblay's. The fatal difference in politics, wrote Fanny, coloured all her father's thinking. But a second visit went more happily. D'Arblay arrived for tea, 'light, gay and palpably in inward spirits'. Dr Burney, stiff and forbidding at first, unbent as the conversation turned to books and he found a fellow bibliophile in d'Arblay. He was soon producing treasures from his book-lined study:

'His fine editions of Ariosto, Dante, Petrarch & Tasso were appreciated with delight. Then came forth select Prints &c. & then the collection of French Classics which gave birth to disquisitions, interrogatories & literary contentions of the gayest & most entertaining nature: – while – though not a word passed between us, I received by every opportunity, *des regards si touchans, si heureux!*

'Ah, my dearest Susanna!' concluded Fanny, 'with a Mind thus formed to meet mine – would my dearest father listen ONLY TO HIMSELF how blest would be my lot!'

As hopes of the counter-revolution in France receded d'Arblay grew dejected. He had called twice on Villiers with his plans for an emigrant corps unsuccessfully; though Villiers, on a third occasion, had promised to pass his memorandum on, he had heard nothing more and was beginning to lose hope of ever doing so. With his prospects more dubious than ever, he wondered for a moment whether Fanny's hesitations stemmed less from prudence than a change of heart. Fanny abandoned all evasions. It was not so, she assured him in a touching letter. Her hesitations were for him, not her. She longed for him to stay in England but she wished him someone younger, prettier, richer – she could not say more alike in heart and mind since that, she imagined, would be impossible.

D'Arblay's answer was equally direct. If tomorrow he had a fortune, he wrote, he would lay it at her feet. His greatest pride would be to share it with her, his greatest happiness would be to minister to hers. It was for her, and her alone, to decide – he himself had nothing to offer and no certainties for the future. He had never asked her what money she had – it was for her to decide if she had the courage to envisage a life together. As for himself, he would always have enough.

There was no longer any question of their love for one another. It was time to turn to ways and means – to Fanny's pension of £100 which, with £20 a year from her literary earnings, was her sole fortune. She could have no expectations from her father in his lifetime; it was far from certain that d'Arblay, a political undesirable in England, would ever find employment there. Their best hope seemed to lie in Fanny's pen: 'Print, print, print,' urged her sister from the country. Meanwhile premature gossip could be damaging. Discretion was essential, especially where Madame de Staël and her friends were concerned. At evenings with the Locks in London, where the Juniperians were frequent callers, Fanny took care to keep her feelings hidden. D'Arblay did the same. 'He made me a distant and ceremonious bow,' wrote Fanny of one such occasion, 'but never once spoke to me except absolutely forced by something incidental. At dinner, also, he never any way addressed me, save once to pick me out an Orange!'

Chapter 9

As on her previous visit to London, Madame de Staël had filled her time to overflowing with engagements. Bollman, who came to call on her, was given audience while she changed between two appointments. Dressed only in her petticoat, she launched into a flood of praises of Narbonne – Bollman was still touchy on the subject – and twirling a scrap of paper, which she was never without, between her fingers as she talked. (One of the few recorded moments of understanding between Madame de Staël and Captain Phillips was when the Captain, seeing her momentarily at a loss for a piece of paper to play with, cut up an envelope and silently handed it to her.) She visited the theatre where Mrs Siddons was performing; she would recall the extraordinary force and freedom of her acting, so different from the formality of French theatrical convention, in her novel *Corinne*. She was received by the Blue Stockings, that coterie of intellectual ladies whose leader, the celebrated Mrs Montagu, had ruled in literary London circles for the last thirty years. 'Brilliant in diamonds, solid in judgement and critical in talk', as Fanny Burney described her, she must have been a worthy foil for the ambassadress, though no record, alas, remains of the encounter.

Politically she had had to watch her step. The war with France had finally split the Whig party, already deeply divided by the

Revolution. Those who, in the words of Talleyrand, 'remained faithful to the cause of liberty despite the mask of blood and filth with which its features have been obscured' were regarded almost as traitors. Faced with war abroad and fear of popular unrest at home, most Whigs had joined ranks with the ruling Tory party. It was left to Charles James Fox and some fifty supporters to stand out against repression and continue to press for peace with France. Madame de Staël was welcomed politely by members of the 'converted opposition' – that is, those Whigs who had seceded to the Tory party – but always with reservations where her politics were concerned. She called on Fox, a meeting she recalled in her history of the Revolution.* But she dared not meet more radical figures such as Sheridan and Grey. 'One might as well throw oneself into the Thames,' she wrote to Gibbon. She yielded to none in her admiration for the British parliamentary system – it had after all been a model for the constitutionalists in France. But at a time when independent speech was stifled and the ruling party reigned supreme, she confessed to finding London the most boring city in the world.

It was a dispirited little band that returned to Juniper Hall towards the end of April. The failure of Dumouriez's initiative, putting an end to all hopes of a counter-revolution, had condemned them once more to inactivity. There was nothing to do but watch and wait while France slipped deeper into anarchy and faction.

Their presence in England was barely tolerated. Their resources were dwindling ominously. Narbonne had arranged for the sale of the few remaining valuables which Madame de Staël had shipped from France before his Paris house had been sequestered by the state. Nothing had struck her more, wrote Fanny Burney, than the firmness and calmness with which he had parted with these debris of his former splendour; 'I assure you it has been for me a proof of his greatness of soul.' Talleyrand had been forced to move to cheaper lodgings and to put his precious library on the market. The books were auctioned at the London house of Messrs Leigh and Sotheby on 12 April, over a nine-day period, but the proceeds brought him little

*'Mr Fox told me, in England in 1793, that at the time of the flight to Varennes he wished the royal family had been allowed to leave and the Constituent Assembly had declared a republic.'

joy. 'Today, with my books sold, I am worth £750 sterling outside France,' he wrote to Madame de Staël. 'What use is that?'

D'Arblay had lingered on in London a few days longer than his friends. He returned to Juniper Hall on foot, arriving in the midst of dinner. Susanna Phillips was dining there with her husband and her small son Norbury. 'We were all instantly on *our* feet to receive him,' she told her sister. 'Norbury danced round & embraced him – M: de N. with the most tender affection put his arms round him & kissed him on each cheek – even Mad^e de Staël put out her fair hand.'

With none of Fanny's prudish reservations, Susanna Phillips was continuing to delight in her French neighbours' company and they in hers. Their sophistication held no fears for her. Like her sister she had been brought up in the brilliant and lively circle surrounding her father, himself the most attractive of companions. 'My heart goes out to Burney,' said Dr Johnson, and Johnson had been only one of the lions that gathered in her father's drawing room. 'Burney's social position,' wrote Macaulay, 'was very peculiar. He belonged in fortune and station to the middle class . . . Yet few nobles could assemble in the most stately mansions of Grosvenor Square or Saint James's Square a society so various and brilliant as was sometimes to be found in Dr Burney's cabin.'

Madame de Staël was always something of a *grande dame*. 'For me,' she once said loftily, 'mankind begins at baron.' But the aristocracy of the intellect had special claims. Dr Burney's encyclopedic *History of Music*, completed four years earlier, had won him European fame. Susanna's intelligence and graceful manners were a recommendation in themselves. She provided too a necessary female presence – Madame de Staël remained uneasily conscious of the proprieties – and could be turned to in domestic difficulties. There had been trouble with the English servants at Juniper Hall. Madame de Staël had brought her own maid, Narbonne's faithful valet and his secretary Ferdinand had followed him from France, but local staff had proved less satisfactory. Susanna, Mrs Lock and even Fanny Burney had been brought into the search for a new maid. 'M. de Narbonne is delighted at your kindness *en vous mêlant de cette affaire*,' wrote Susanna when Fanny produced a suitable candidate, 'and comically assures me that the damsel whose reply they await tho' not perhaps as *tall* is as *ugly* as the one you have found for them.'

For Narbonne Susanna was 'the sweetest, the most intelligent' of companions, her gentle ways at times a soothing contrast to those of his more brilliant mistress. Eight years later, when the consumption which had always threatened her health brought about her early death, he would greet the news with an agony of weeping. For d'Arblay Susanna had always had a special feeling. Less worldly than Talleyrand and Narbonne, he fitted naturally into her household and her sister's unresolved romance had brought him even nearer. Already her children had christened him with the pet name of Tio and d'Arblay, when no one was near, took pleasure in calling her '*ma petite soeur*'.

Captain Phillips, for the time being, suspected nothing of the intrigue brewing between d'Arblay and his sister-in-law. But he got on well with d'Arblay, with whom he used to practise fencing, and d'Arblay as a gallant soldier appreciated stories of the Captain's adventurous past. A former officer of the Marines, Phillips had sailed with Captain Cook on his last voyage, narrowly escaping death at the time of Cook's murder by the natives of Hawaii. He had distinguished himself on this occasion by his bravery in rescuing a fellow sailor who had got into difficulties while they were swimming back to their ship, and though badly wounded himself succeeded in bringing him on board. Since then he had served as a soldier and was now retired on half pay; he would abandon his commission altogether at the end of 1797.

There was a special poignance for Mrs Phillips as she watched her sister's love affair unfold. Her own marriage was becoming increasingly unhappy. Ostensibly it had been a good match. Captain Phillips had estates in Ireland, his father had been the illegitimate but acknowledged son of the Irish Viscount Molesworth. But he had proved to be hopelessly unreliable about money. His Irish property was mortgaged to the hilt and he had borrowed considerable sums from Dr Burney on which he could not even pay the interest. Behind a bluff and jovial exterior lay a truculent and unstable streak which would grow worse as his money troubles deepened.

Except to her father and her sister, Mrs Phillips kept her troubles to herself. At Juniper Hall her husband was a welcome guest and a genial host at their cottage in return. Her letters continue their saga of impromptu visits and the comings and goings of other French visitors, each with their share of news and information. It was pleasant to pass on compliments about d'Arblay to her sister. 'I was pleased to hear M: de N. speak of his friend with the greatest affection and esteem,' she told her, '& Mad^e de Staël allowing of all the praise he bestowed on him: "It would be impossible to find a man of purer sentiments of honour, loyalty and friendship – generous to the point of quixotry – equally good in company – even tempered, cheerful, kind – *enfin c'est un bien bon enfant*."'

There were compliments too for Fanny Burney as Madame de Staël discussed her novels. (She would later class *Cecilia* with such masterpieces as the *Princesse de Clèves* in her *Essai sur les Fictions*.) It was Fanny's power to invent a complex and yet natural story which she most admired and in which she felt most lacking. Over coffee one evening she sketched out the plot of one of her own novels, probably *Pauline*, published three years later, in which the heroine, having been seduced in early youth, suffers agonies of remorse and shame, eventually dying of sorrow at her unworthiness of the man she loves. Would Fanny have dared to treat of such a subject, she asked Susanna.

'I don't know if she would have *dared*,' replied Susanna laughing, 'but I don't think she would have *wished* to.'

Madame de Staël, a little piqued, replied that her mother, a woman of the austerest morals, had read the book and found nothing to object to in it. Since Madame Necker, in the words of a contemporary, had been dipped in starch at birth, the argument seemed conclusive.

Madame de Staël was beginning to be irritated by the prudery of Fanny Burney which, as she already half suspected, lay behind her reluctance to pursue their friendship. She had been greatly hurt and disappointed by Fanny's avoidance of her company, Susanna told her sister, and was on the verge of being offended. When she asked whether Fanny Burney would be staying with the Locks on their return from London, Susanna – who knew her sister had no intention of staying at Norbury Park while Madame de Staël remained next door – was forced to answer that Dr Burney could not spare her. Madame de Staël was amazed: 'Is a woman a minor for ever in your country?' she asked Susanna. 'It seems to me that your sister is like a girl of fourteen.' Susanna did her best to enlarge on the constraints unmarried women faced in England, but it was evident that Madame de Staël did not believe her.

On one point, however, Susanna Phillips was able to reassure her sister. Despite d'Arblay's frequent disappearances to London, the Juniperians, she was convinced, knew nothing of the reason for them. It was true that Talleyrand once said he suspected him of being in love, and that Madame de Staël had said he was becoming quite a Londoner, but beyond that they had not speculated. They had other things on their mind.

Unwillingly Madame de Staël had determined to return to Switzerland. After two months of unsuccessful negotiations with the revolutionary government, her husband had been withdrawn from Paris; the failure of Dumouriez's initiative had put an end to all immediate hopes of a treaty between France and Sweden. Temporarily unoccupied, he was planning to join his parents-in-law in Switzerland. Once away from Paris and its dangers, there could be no good reason why his wife should not join him there. In any case her position in England was becoming untenable. Fanny Burney's attitude was symptomatic. She could have no illusions either as to the political hatreds she aroused.

Over the previous three years Madame de Staël, like most other prominent figures of the time, had grown used to every kind of scurrilous attack in the French press. But in England, where she might have hoped for understanding, she felt the injustice of being used as a scapegoat for the Revolution's horrors and excesses. Amongst the papers left behind at Juniper Hall (which were later preserved amongst the Burney archives) is the draft of a statement which never saw the light of day but which can be seen, in a way, as her apologia.

'I cannot believe,' she wrote, 'that in an enlightened country such as England the opinions of a few young women can be ranked amongst the causes of a revolution prepared over the centuries and welcomed by more than twenty million people. I do not know at what stage in such a story the faults or qualities of a woman find their place. Those who believe in their influence can only have followed the progress of the Revolution at balls and routs; their conclusions must appear ridiculous to English philosophers . . . I have never had any contacts with the republican government, now masters in France, beyond having the courage to defy their menaces and to use my special position to snatch a few victims from their clutches. At other times this might have been enough to arouse a certain sympathy; today it is not even sufficient to save me from calumny.

'But why talk of myself,' she concluded. 'Let us set aside personal considerations. The misfortunes of others demand my attention and these cruel distractions must take precedence over my own.'

Meanwhile, with her departure from England inevitable, she must make certain that she would have a refuge for her friends in Switzerland. Those who, like Montmorency, had gone to claim their property in France were increasingly at risk. Talleyrand in London was living on a knife-edge, watched and suspected by the authorities who saw him as a 'deep and dangerous man'. Madame de Staël had never wavered in her passion for Narbonne, but she had always been catholic in her affections and Talleyrand, whatever his later feelings, had found her friendship his chief solace while he was in England. 'It is absolutely certain,' he wrote to her after she left, 'that whatever I have been able to preserve of decency and good humour is due entirely to our union – and you know what I mean by *our*.'

There would certainly be a place for Talleyrand in Switzerland. As for Narbonne, she regarded his departure as a natural conse-quence of hers. She wrote anxiously to Gibbon in Switzerland to see what the attitude of the Swiss authorities towards him would be. He must realize, she told him, that the Revolution had swept all normal conventions away and that her love for Narbonne, sanctified by five years of shared ideals and dangers, had become an irrevocable fact of life. The Swiss authorities, however, might not see her friendship in the same exalted light; moreover, the bailiff of Lausanne, a determined aristocrat, was far from sympathetic to the constitution-alists and had no wish to see them settle on his territory. She needed all Gibbon's good influences to obtain permission for her lover's stay. Still more important was the presence of her husband to lend respectability to her establishment. It was essential that he should be there to act as host for Narbonne and her other guests.

Staël, somewhat battered by his recent experiences in Paris, seemed only too happy at the idea of a reconciliation with his wife. Her letters, increasingly affectionate in tone, declared her eagerness for a reunion – she would leave the question of her friends till later. But he flatly refused to come to England to collect her, arranging instead that his secretary, Pierre Signeul, should meet her at Ostend to escort her across Europe. Signeul was to write to her as soon as he reached Ostend and would then await her arrival on the boat from Dover.

It would be two or three months before Madame de Staël could prepare the ground for her lover in Switzerland, even supposing that her husband made no objections. Without her generous contributions it would be impossible to continue the relatively lavish style of entertaining at Juniper Hall. The flow of visitors would have to cease, and in order to save the expenses of a cook it was agreed that Narbonne and d'Arblay should take their main meal each day at Mrs Phillips's cottage once the ambassadress had left. Susanna was delighted to help out, Captain Phillips was agreeable, but she was worried how to break the news to Dr Burney. It was certain he would disapprove unless the *ménagèreship*, as she called it, was tactfully explained. She begged her sister's help in composing an appropriate letter. It was, she felt, still more important to Fanny than herself that their father should be propitiated, though Madame de Staël's impending departure removed at least the worst of his objections to her neighbours.

Chapter 10

Throughout her time in England, as a running accompaniment to her social activities, Madame de Staël had been busy writing. The major part of her essay *De l'Influence des passions sur le bonheur des individus et des nations*, her first major work, was written at Juniper Hall. D'Arblay had made it his chosen task to copy out what she had written, transcribing her almost indecipherable writing into his neat and regular hand. In the evenings there would be readings from the work in progress.

The book was not published until 1795 and its political section – the influence of the passions upon nations – was never written, though its main themes were set out in the introduction. Begun in the wake of the September massacres and completed after the Terror, the essay reflected something of the anguish her country was experiencing. On a more personal level, above all in the chapter on love, it bore the imprint of her relationship with Narbonne, still superficially happy but already showing signs of stress. In paragraph after paragraph she descanted on the inequalities of men's and women's fate:

'Nature and society have disinherited one half of mankind; strength, courage, independence, all belong to men; and if they surround our youth with homage it is only to procure the amusement of overthrowing our empire.'

Bitterly she observed the double standard of which her stay in England had made her specially aware: 'Love is the sole passion of a woman . . . The history of a woman's life is an episode in that of a man. Reputation, honour, esteem, everything depends on the conduct which women observe in this connection; even the laws of morality in the eyes of the world seem suspended in the relations between men and women . . . A man may have received from a woman marks of devotion which would bind two friends, two comrades in arms together and would dishonour the one who was capable of forgetting them . . . and discount them all, in attributing them to love, as though one sentiment, one further gift, diminished the price of all the others.'

And in her chapter on vanity she summed up what would always be a central sorrow: 'The appearance of a woman, whatever the power and breadth of her mind, whatever the importance of the affairs with which she is concerned, will always be a drawback or an advantage in the story of her life; it is men that wish it so.' She would have given everything, a friend remarked, to be a beauty, and it is revealing that the heroines of her novels, so like her in other respects, are always endowed with beauty as well.

Fanny Burney, no longer blind to her relations with Narbonne, saw her character with a novelist's eye. There is surely something of Madame de Staël in her novel *The Wanderer*, when the ugly eccentric Elinor Joddrel inveighs against the conventions which deny her the right to express her emotions as freely as a man:

'Why, for so many centuries has man, alone, been supposed to possess, not only force and power for action, but even all the rights of taste; all the fine sensibilities which impel our happiest sympathies in the choice of our life's partners? Why, not alone, is woman to be excluded from the exertions of courage, the field of glory, the immortal death of honour; – not alone to be denied deliberating upon the safety of the state of which she is a member . . . must even her heart be circumscribed by boundaries as narrow as her sphere of action in life? Must she be taught to subdue all its natural emotions? To hide them as sin and deny them as shame . . . Must nothing that is spontaneous, generous, intuitive, spring from her soul to her lips?'

Juniper Hall around
1800 (artist unknown)

Juniper Hall in 1844,
from a watercolour by
Dibdin

Fanny Burney reading, from a pencil drawing by her cousin Edward Burney

Susanna Phillips, from a miniature

Fanny Burney after her marriage

William Lock, by Edward Burney from a
portrait by Thomas Lawrence

Mrs Lock, by Dowman

Madame de Staël, after a portrait by Gérard

Talleyrand, after a portrait by Gérard

Louis de Narbonne, from a contemporary portrait

Mathieu de Montmorency, from a contemporary engraving

Alexandre d'Arblay, a crayon drawing probably by William Lock, Jr

Madame de Staël in conversation, a contemporary engraving

Mrs Phillips' cottage, c. 1905, by
Ellen Hill

Norbury Park, from a contemporary
print

The painted drawing room at Norbury Park

The drawing room at Juniper Hall

The contrasted heroine of *The Wanderer*, needless to say, is impeccably modest in her behaviour and fortunately for her very pretty as well, but Fanny at least saw the problems of the passionate Elinor Joddrel.

Meanwhile, her own quiet idyll was progressing. Forty years had widened her knowledge of the world, but her decorous exterior still hid a youthfully romantic heart. D'Arblay had one to match it, though his experience of manners and morals in France had been very different from hers. As a young man he had been a friend and fellow officer of Choderlos de Laclos. He had published a set of mildly amorous verses under the pseudonym of the Chevalier d'Anceny; Laclos had borrowed the name for one of his characters in *Les Liaisons Dangereuses*. But he had none of the cynicism of his notorious contemporary. A high sense of honour had sustained him through his military career; it had earned him the trust and friendship of Lafayette and Narbonne, and even of the King, who created him a Chevalier of Saint Louis, his personal order of chivalry, not long before his downfall. Fanny's previous romances had been tepid affairs which had never quite come to the boil; they had left her wounded and humiliated. D'Arblay's gallantry and ardour were a new experience; she was deeply moved too by his misfortunes, his diffidence, his fortitude. And d'Arblay, whose first glimpses of English life had been with the Locks and the Phillipses, saw Fanny in the settings where she was happiest. In their exchange of themes, in the enchanted evenings at Norbury Park and Juniper Hall, he had come to know and appreciate her qualities of heart and mind. Had it not been for the Locks, Mrs Phillips – and one other person – d'Arblay told her, he would have been quite tired of life in the first despairing months in England.

It was to the Locks that he and Fanny turned for counsel as they contemplated the practical problems that lay before them. William Lock was now a rich man; the illegitimate but only child of a wealthy banker, he had inherited a fortune on his father's death. But he had not always been rich; as a young man he had known poverty and he had no romantic illusions about it. D'Arblay's memorandum for Villiers had gone unanswered (though Villiers later followed the recommendations he had made). In the political climate of the time

Mr Lock could see no other chance of finding him an honourable employment. Any hopes of a pension for his past services in France must depend on the overthrow of the revolutionary government, an uncertain prospect at best. As Narbonne's friend and former chief of staff d'Arblay could always be certain of sharing his fortunes, but Madame de Staël's impending departure made it likely that Narbonne would follow her to Switzerland. If d'Arblay married Fanny he must stay behind.

Fanny's pension from the Queen remained the key to the future. Would the Queen withdraw it in disapproval of her marriage? To ask her beforehand might precipitate an unfavourable answer. Tactfully Fanny was preparing the ground in letters describing d'Arblay's admirable qualities to friends in the royal household; she knew it was likely that her letters would be read to the Queen. If her pension were retained, thought Mr Lock, she and d'Arblay might survive on £120 a year 'as many a curate does'. They would have to live carefully, he admitted. One day's roast must appear cold the next day and hashed the day after. But d'Arblay, he was certain, could happily live on bread and water; as for Fanny, he told Mrs Phillips, 'you know an egg is a great dinner for her.'

After nearly thirty years of marriage Mr Lock remained a firm believer in true love. Almost wistfully, in her essay on the passions Madame de Staël describes a walk with two English friends (the Locks) in the woods near Norbury Park. They passed an encampment of gipsies whose miserable state, ragged, homeless and exposed to all weathers, made her exclaim in pity. 'All the same,' said Lock, with a gesture to his wife, 'if in order to be united with her I had been obliged to submit to such a state I would gladly have begged my bread for thirty years.' 'Ah yes,' echoed his wife, 'even then we would have been the happiest of beings.' These words, wrote Madame de Staël, had remained engraved on her heart.

In London the Locks' drawing room in Portland Place continued to provide a sympathetic meeting place for Fanny and her suitor. Since the end of April Fanny had come there for a lengthy stay. Mrs Lock and her daughters, Amelia and Augusta, had caught measles; Amelia and Augusta were seriously and at one time dangerously ill. Fanny was well accustomed to sickbeds; unmarried amidst a tribe of relations, she had always been much in demand in the family crises and the sudden illnesses, so much more alarming than they would be now, which occurred from time to time.

Much occupied with nursing, she still had time to see d'Arblay, who came whenever he could to see her and to ask about the invalids. He talked too of his hopes and plans, at one moment full of optimism, at others close to despair at the difficulties that confronted them. A violent attack on Lafayette and his officers in a royalist paper, *Le Peltier*, cast him into especial gloom. Pamphlets, broadsheets and newspapers abounded amongst the émigré community in London. Peltier's pamphlets, published monthly, were amongst the most widely read of these. In this particular issue, attacking Lafayette for his arrogance and ambition, Peltier denounced his officers for their cowardice and cupidity and the constitutionalists in general for the fatal half-measures which had made them, as he wrote, 'mere abortions of the Revolution'.

D'Arblay, Fanny told her sister, had had 'not a moment's rest from cruel indignation' and had devoted every minute since to preparing a reply which, poor as he was, he intended to publish at his own expense. He came to seek out Fanny Burney and Mr Lock to read them what he had written. He found them in the drawing room with Mr Lock's two sons.

'What a reading then followed,' wrote Fanny, ' . . . What noble integrity, how pure a sense of Honour, what disinterested Patriotism & what courage in Misfortune were alternately portrayed! But when, in coming home to his more immediate position he suddenly averts to a village in which *des NOUVEAUX AMIS* had once more endeared life to him, & would make him a new HOME, to enable him to support his exile from his lost country . . . I could with difficulty keep my seat. My cheeks burnt, my Eyes filled, my heart palpitated, & I pulled my Bonnet veil over my face and leant my head on my hand. I do not believe I could else have remained in the room.'

Fanny's confusion, under the curious gaze of Mr Lock's two sons, was genuine. While Mr Lock discussed d'Arblay's article and its presentation – d'Arblay, much agitated, pacing up and down or flinging himself despondently on the sofa – she found herself almost unable to speak. 'A confirmation so exquisitely delicious to me of his real decision to fix in England – and at Mickleham! at my Susan's & my Norbury Park – My heart was so full, so full – of pity for Him, and of gratitude with Pleasure that, since I could not express – yet knew not how to conceal my feelings, I wished to leave the room and be alone.'

Back in London for a final visit, Madame de Staël came to see the Locks, this time to say goodbye. The date of her departure was not yet fixed, but she would be awaiting a message from her husband at Juniper Hall. Perhaps she would see the Locks again at Norbury Park; if not, she told them, she would live on her memories. Some of the sweetest moments of her life had been spent beneath their roof.

Fanny Burney, who had been busy in the sickroom upstairs, was called down by Mr Lock to come and take her leave of Madame de Staël. She found her in the drawing room, sublime on a sofa, and in a far from easy mood. Half playfully, half angrily, she began to attack Fanny for her secession from her friendship and to demand her reasons. Fanny, putting as good a face on things as possible, declared she was not at liberty to reveal them and an energetic argument ensued, 'provoking and threatening' on the ambassadress's side and on Fanny's 'partly sportive and partly obsequiously begging for mercy'. D'Arblay, looking on in the intervals of talking to another guest, could only exclaim, '*O mon Dieu! mon Dieu!*,' in a tone of weary restraint. As the party left to go, seeing d'Arblay stay behind, the ambassadress shot him a look of 'meaning wickedness'. 'I am sure her suspicions are strong,' wrote Fanny.

Madame de Staël had no intention of letting matters rest. At Juniper Hall, he told Fanny ruefully, she tormented d'Arblay with her '*plaisanteries*' and a few days later when she saw him writing a joint note to Fanny Burney with Mrs Phillips, she insisted on adding her own postcript. 'Tell me,' she wrote, 'if you've discovered any further secrets since I saw you – as for me, I assure you that I love you and give you full permission to publish the fact.' Thirty years later, in annotating the letter, Fanny's embarrassment still showed: 'The *secrets* meant were F.B.'s motives for declining visits to Juniper, the abode of Mme de Staël. F.B. had received *renseignements* which she durst not avow, but which forced her to stop the peculiar intimacy which the charm of Mme de Staël had brought on, in F.B.'s ignorance of the unhappy incorrectness at least of that wonderful (enchanting) highly gifted woman.' Embarrassed or not, Fanny Burney's prudery was adamant. With the perilous course of her own marriage to chart in the face of the world's, her father's, and probably the Queen's disapproval, she could afford no concessions on the way.

Chapter 11

———————— ❧ ————————

As soon as Mrs Lock and her daughters were well enough to travel they left London to convalesce at Norbury Park. Despite repeated invitations Fanny Burney did not accompany them. She was afraid of a confrontation with Madame de Staël; she would not come to Surrey till the ambassadress had left. But she thought wistfully of the country. 'Did the Wood look very beautiful?' she wrote to Mrs Lock from London. 'I have figured it to myself; with the three dear Convalescents wandering in its winding paths & inhaling its freshness . . . I wanted prodigiously to have issued forth from some green recess to have hailed your return.'

London seemed cramped and airless. Her mind was a turmoil of uncertainties about her marriage. As she had so often done as a child, she took herself to a familiar refuge in the country. Chessington Hall, near Leatherhead, had been the home of Fanny's second father, her 'dear Daddy Crisp', as she called him. An intimate friend of the Burney family, it had been he who had encouraged her first literary efforts. It was round the mulberry tree in his garden that Fanny, then aged twenty-five, had danced for joy when she heard of *Evelina*'s success. He had died some years before but the house was still running as a kind of boarding house, kept by two old ladies who had been his legatees.

Crisp had been something of a recluse, soured by failures in the London world of letters, and his house, in the depths of Surrey, was as lonely and remote as it was possible to imagine. It was approached by a cart track over a common which was often impassable in bad weather and would shake the stoutest wagon even in good. But Fanny loved the house, with its memories of her old friend, its nooks and crannies and dark passages 'leading to nothing', its tapestries and blue-and-white-tiled fireplaces, and its elderly hostesses, Kitty Cooke and Mrs Hamilton, who welcomed her visit with delight. It was here that in the past she had taken herself to write *Cecilia*, her second novel, in peace and quiet, and that she now hoped to compose her thoughts. There was much to think about. D'Arblay's bleak prospects of employment, the unlikelihood that things would ever change in France, left all hopes of a solution to their problems in her hands. 'Print, print, print,' her sister had urged her. Already before leaving London she had written to d'Arblay of her hopes of starting a new novel which could be published with his help in both English and French. At Chessington Hall she could begin to undertake the project.

But the inspiration which had all but run away with her pen when she wrote her earlier novels seemed to have deserted her.

'Do you know anything of a certain young lady who eludes all my enquiries, famous for having eight sisters, all of uncommon talents?' she wrote to Mrs Lock. 'Whether she is offended that I have slighted her offers so long, or whether she is fickle, or only whimsical, I know not. All that is quite undoubted is, that she has concealed herself so effectively from my researches, that I might as well look for Justice & Clemency from the French Convention, as for this former friend in the plains and lanes of Chesington, where, erst, she met me whether I would or no!'

Madame de Staël was still at Juniper Hall when the Locks returned. So delighted was she at the news that she insisted on calling on them on the very day of their arrival. Susanna Phillips, who had done her best to dissuade her, went ahead to warn the Locks of her impending visit. Mr Lock, she reported, looked 'quite *abattu*' at the prospect, while his wife and daughters, already worn out by their journey, decided to take the line of least resistance and disappear to their rooms before she came. Meeting Madame de Staël with Narbonne in their carriage at the foot of Norbury Hill as she was returning, Susanna made one last attempt to delay them. But the ambassadress, quite undeterred, declared they would call on Lock by himself and drove on up the hill.

The Locks had been full of gratitude for Fanny's nursing, Susanna told her sister. 'I have no time to tell you how our sweet Friend expressed her delight in yr Nursing of them . . . she says you *slaved* for them, & that kindness was too common a word to use &c &c in speaking of your exertions.' As for d'Arblay, he was impatient to see Fanny again, though he understood her reasons for staying away.

'I pray you, my dearest friend,' he wrote, 'to make your disposals in such a manner that you could very soon take care of your beloved and not yet quite recovered sicks. Don't forget another ill who want's very much his amiable physician . . . Come Come my dear *Cecilia*, Come and be my indulgent master. Don't forget your grateful scholar. It is so *intéressant* for him to make all his utmost endeavours in order to improve his broken english! Come, I pray you, with all my heart!'

He sent her a favourite pen which he had had for twenty-one years and Fanny made much of his gift in her answering note:

'Come little Pen! & tell me what you have been doing these 21 years past? Will you serve me as you have served your late Possessor? . . . Will you remind me of your Right Owner, by disdaining to transmit to Paper one Sentiment that has not Truth for its basis, & Honour for its principle? O little Pen! – if after your long service you degenerate from that noble simplicity – I reject you with aversion. – But if, on the contrary, you fulfil my just expectations, I will keep – & use – & cherish you for ever.'

Despite these delightful exchanges d'Arblay's spirits were low, his head tormented with one project after another, only to be rejected on the grounds of impracticality. '*Je suis – tout à fait –* disheartened,' he told Mrs Phillips, as he described the failure of his initiative with Villiers. 'I can do nothing . . . you can imagine the position I am in.'

He had thought of asking Lock to recommend him as a tutor to some young man of family who planned to enter a military career, but Lock, alas, had no such contacts. He even thought of writing to the Queen, to ask her approval of the marriage. Fanny exclaimed at the impossibility of such a suggestion, which even d'Arblay realized was far-fetched. In all her time in the royal household Fanny had never made any direct solicitation; such a thing would be quite contrary to etiquette for anyone in daily attendance on the Queen. Dr Burney, who had hoped for some possible benefit for his family, had been sadly disappointed on this score. As for d'Arblay, she knew that any further mention of a Frenchman at this moment would be bound to incur displeasure.

Meanwhile, as long as Madame de Staël remained at Juniper Hall, d'Arblay was in a state of suspended animation. Conscious of his self-imposed obligations, he was working night and day to complete his task of copying her essay on the passions. He joined in too in various expeditions to their neighbours, the Locks first of all but other local magnates as well. News of the '*ménagèreship*' had got round locally and Mrs Phillips describes a call from a neighbour, Miss Filewood, on an afternoon when the Juniperians had gone to visit the famous landscape gardens of Paines Hill, taking her small son Norbury with them. Miss Filewood was ostensibly calling about raising subscriptions on behalf of the exiled French clergy in England. But she was hoping to indulge her curiosity as well and having talked briefly of the colony at Juniper Hall moved abruptly to the '*ménagèreship*':

'So, Mrs Phillips, we hear you are to have Mr Norbone and the other French company to live with you – Pray is it so?'

Mrs Phillips, somewhat taken aback, replied as composedly as she could that Madame de Staël was leaving for Switzerland in the next few days. As only Narbonne and d'Arblay, for whom she and her husband felt a real friendship and esteem, would be left at Juniper Hall, they had offered them their hospitality for a while to save them the trouble and expense of housekeeping.

At this point the party from Paines Hill arrived. Miss Filewood, wrote Mrs Phillips, obliged them with another two hours of her company though she had already taken tea, and despite the fact that everyone was talking English, proceeded to question Narbonne in abominable French:

'*Je vous prie, M. Gnawbone, comment se porte la Reine?*'

'Her pronunciation was such,' wrote Mrs Phillips, 'that I thought his understanding her miraculous: however he answered with his accustomed *douceur* and politeness that he hoped well, but had no means but general ones of information.

'"I believe," said she afterwards, "nobody was so hurt at the King's death but my papa! He couldn't ride on horseback the next day!"

'She then told M. de Narbonne some anecdotes (very new to him, no doubt) which she had read in the newspapers of the Convention and then spoke of M. Egalité. "I hope," said she, flinging out her arms with great violence, "he'll come to be gullytined. He showed the King how to be gullytined; so now I hope he'll be gullytined himself!"

'If the subject of her vehemence and blunders had been less melancholy,' concluded Mrs Phillips, 'I know not how I should have kept my countenance.'

The rest of this evening, once this '*bête personnage*' was gone, was very pleasant: 'Madame de Staël is, with all her wildness and blemishes a very delightful companion, and M. de N. rises upon me in esteem and affection every time I see him.'

Madame de Staël made no secret of her reluctance to leave England and complained bitterly of her husband's lack of consideration in not coming to fetch her himself. But she made the most of her remaining time, her gaiety and sparkle undiminished as long as there were friends around her. Mrs Phillips, calling at Norbury Park after church one Sunday, found all the Juniperians there and listened to one of the best conversations she had ever heard on literary subjects, with Madame de Staël, Talleyrand, a visiting Swiss man of letters, Etienne Dumont, and Lock as the chief speakers. Mrs Phillips, obliged to return to her 'miserable dinner', could hardly tear herself away.

On the following evening the Phillipses were dining at Juniper Hall when an express letter arrived for Madame de Staël. She read it with a change in her expression that made it easy for her guests to guess the contents. It was from her husband's secretary, Pierre Signeul, who had arrived in Ostend and was now awaiting her in order to escort her back to Switzerland. Madame de Staël had

86

intended to walk home with her guests in the moonlight but felt too overcome to do so. D'Arblay accompanied the Phillipses home while Narbonne remained behind to comfort her.

The next day, Tuesday, 21 May, they all met again at Norbury Park to spend her final day together. Madame de Staël, wrote Susanna, could not rally her spirits at all and seemed like one torn from all that was dear to her. After many entreaties to Susanna to look after the friends she was leaving she added a message for her sister:

'And tell Miss Burney I don't hold anything against her – I leave this country loving her sincerely and without the slightest ill will.'

'I assured her earnestly,' wrote Susanna, 'and with more words than I have room to insert, not only of your admiration but affection, and sensibility of her worth, and chagrin at seeing no more of her. I hope I exceeded not your wishes; *mais il n'y avait pas moyen de résister.*'

Madame de Staël seemed pleased by Susanna's assurances. 'You are very good to say so,' she said in a low voice and dropped the subject.

D'Arblay left the party early in order to finish his work of copying the last few pages of Madame de Staël's manuscript. Narbonne and Mrs Phillips accompanied her back to Juniper Hall. She sobbed aloud in saying goodbye to Mrs Lock and continued sobbing half way down the hill; her parting with Mrs Phillips was equally affecting. The next morning, determined to catch one last glimpse of her, Mrs Phillips stationed herself outside the village school where her coach would pass, with a little present and a farewell note. Madame de Staël was too overcome to speak but kissed her hand to her through the window 'with a very speaking and touching expression of countenance'.

Narbonne accompanied his mistress to Dover, pausing to stay the night with Talleyrand in London, and another with Lally Tollendal. On the evening of 25 May they parted at Dover, where Madame de Staël was due to catch the night boat for Ostend. Whatever the ups and downs of their English interlude had been, their last moments together were full of emotion, both lovers perhaps remembering their parting in Paris, nine months before, when Madame de Staël, with death in her heart, had said goodbye to Narbonne not knowing if she would ever see him again. Narbonne swore that his life belonged to her, that he would never forget what she had done for him, and promised to join her in Switzerland as soon as she sent for him. Much moved, but sustained by the thought of their reunion, she set out for Ostend and the difficult journey ahead.

Her final note was to her friends at Norbury Park. 'I shall think myself happy if my name is mentioned with regret in one of the evening gatherings at Norbury. Adieu, Madame, if distances vanish under the gentle influence of memory, you may imagine that this letter is dated from Juniper Hall.'

Chapter 12

Madame de Staël reached Ostend on the afternoon of 27 May after a stormy crossing. 'I thought of what you had suffered,' she told Narbonne. She arrived in the midst of dramatic happenings in France, made more immediate by her closeness to the theatre of events. In England the news had been muted by the difficulties of communication and the sense of distance provided by the Channel. Here in Ostend, with the Paris papers no more than two or three days old, she could follow what was happening far more closely. Through the last days of May the struggle between the Jacobins and the more moderate Girondins, discredited by Dumouriez's defection and the disastrous progress of the war, was reaching its climax. Madame de Staël held no brief for the Girondins – they had been equally responsible with the Jacobins for the downfall of the monarchy – but she regarded them as the lesser of two evils. By the end of May it was clear that their days were numbered. On 2 June while the Paris mob surrounded the Chamber of Deputies, the Girondins were expelled from the National Convention; a wave of arrests would follow. The reign of terror was beginning.

Madame de Staël would look back on the fourteen months that followed the downfall of the Girondins with a shudder of horror. Even at a distance of more than twenty years, when she wrote her great history of the French Revolution, she could not bear to go into its events in detail. 'It seems that like Dante one descends from circle to circle, plunging ever deeper into the inferno,' she wrote. 'One fears even to embark on such a story, so ineffaceable are the traces of blood it leaves on the imagination.' It was against this background that her letters to Narbonne would be written over the next few months, emotions heightened to an unbearable pitch by what was happening in France.

It is an almost disconcerting change of mood to return to England and Fanny Burney's reaction to her departure. Not surprisingly she felt a certain awkwardness.

'I have regretted excessively the finishing so miserably an acquaintance begun with so much spirit & pleasure & the dépit I fear Mad^e de S[taël] must have experienced,' she wrote to Mrs Lock. 'I wish the World would take more care of itself and less of its neighbours. I should have been *very safe*, I trust, without such flights, & distances, & breaches! . . . I am vexed however – very much vexed at the whole business. I hope she left Norbury Park with full satisfaction with its steady and more *comfortable* connection.'

But there was happier news to relate. D'Arblay, free to move now that Madame de Staël and his work of copying were gone, had lost no time in making an expedition to Chessington to see Fanny, and her description of his visit is as rollicking as a passage from her novels.

Her elderly hostesses – fat, round Mrs Hamilton and her young niece Kitty Cooke, 'only sixty-three, healthy, bonny, plump, merry and comfortable' – had been in a flutter for days at the expected arrival of their visitor.

'Mrs Hamilton ordered half a Ham to be boiled ready; – & Miss Kitty trimmed up her best Cap – & tried it on, on Saturday, to get it in shape to her face. She made Chocolate also, – which we drank up on Monday & Tuesday, because it was spoiling: – "I have never seen none of the French Quality," she says, "and I have a *purdigious Curiosity*; though as to Dukes and Dukes' sons, and these high top Captains, I know they'll think me a mere country Bumpkin . . . "

'Unfortunately, however, when all was prepared above – the French *top captain* entered while poor Miss Kitty was in *dishbill*! & Mrs Hamilton finishing washing up her China from breakfast! A

Maid who was out at the Pump, first saw the arrival, ran in to give Miss Kitty time to escape – for she was in her round dress *nightcap* & without her roll and curls – However he followed too quick – & Mrs Hamilton was seen in her linen gown and mob, though she had put on a silk one in expectation, for every noon these 4 or 5 days past – & Miss Kitty was in such confusion she hurried out of the Room. She soon, however, returned with the roll and curls, & the Forehead & Throat *fashionably lost*, in a silk Gown. – And though she had not intended to speak a word the gentle quietness of her Guest so surprized and pleased her, that she never quitted his side while he stayed and has sung his praises ever since.'

Mrs Hamilton, added Fanny, had shed tears on hearing d'Arblay's history after he had gone. 'She says now she has really seen one of the *French Gentry* that has been drove out of their Country by the villains she has heard of, she shall begin to believe there really has been a Revolution! & Miss Kitty says "I purtest I did not know before but it was all a Sham!"'

D'Arblay, on his return to Juniper Hall, was much less happy with this visit. He had not had a chance to speak to Fanny alone, he complained to Mrs Phillips. His hostesses had never left the room for a moment and Fanny had done nothing but talk of trivialities in English. He was the more disappointed since he had written to her at length two days before, setting out the questions he had been turning over ceaselessly since their last meetings in London. Had Fanny reflected on them during her stay at Chessington? Above all, had she weighed up the difficulties of the restricted existence they would have to lead?

'Forgive me, dear Fanny, but I suspect you are no more versed in the details of housekeeping than I am . . . I'm ready to bear any hardships, and I assure you with all my heart that the most substantial fortune elsewhere doesn't weigh for a moment against the *bare necessities* with *you*, and in the company of our friends. But it is these bare necessities that worry me . . . I would be the most despicable of men if, without having made sure of them, I involved you in misfortunes against which I should no longer have the strength to fight.'

These were serious questions and there were no new answers to them. Before replying to his letter Fanny turned to her most trusted counsellors, her sister and the Locks. She was convinced from d'Arblay's letters that he was desperately dejected when he was alone:

'It is not that he wants patience; it seems a virtue he even eminently possesses: but he wants *rational expectation* of better times: expectation founded on something more than mere aerial *Hope* that builds one day what the next blasts – & then to build again – & again be blasted.'

It would be cruel to encourage him any further in thinking he could find an honourable employment in the present state of things in England; far better to base their hopes on what she had already and the prospect of earning further money by her pen. But nothing could remove the uncertainty about the pension. She did not think it could be taken away: she had been told by her fellow Keeper of the Robes, Mrs Schwellenberg, that it had been given her as compensation for her five years of employment. 'The Queen knows,' she wrote, 'that I left her with only losses and debts.'

In her own mind she was ready, she had always been ready to take the gamble. For the first time in her life she had found a man whom she could love whole-heartedly. The worldly sacrifices she must make, the visits to Court, the comparative comfort of her father's home, seemed nothing in comparison.

Having set out her thoughts to the Locks and her sister, she wrote to d'Arblay even before they answered.

'You desire to know,' she wrote, 'if I have weighed well how I could support an entirely retired life & c –

'Here comes a great YES! I have considered it thoroughly . . . Situation I well know, is wholly powerless to render me either happy or miserable. My peace of mind, my chearfulness of spirits, my every chance of felicity, rest totally & solely upon enjoying the society, the confidence & the kindness of those I esteem & love.'

D'Arblay was deeply touched by her letter. But he was still tortured by scruples. He did not doubt her courage but it would be inexcusable to abuse her generosity by risking her health and well-being. Would even the £120 they might have be enough to provide her with the necessary comforts? And what if some kind friend abused her to the Queen and the pension were withdrawn?

Once more Fanny Burney had no certainties to offer. But she could not bear to see him wasting further time on useless questionings. Some solution must be found, even if it meant abandoning the thought of marriage. Let him seek the advice of Mr Lock, she told him, explaining his anxieties – if Lock thought they were truly justified he would not deceive him. And then . . . 'you can well imagine what I must say next.'

Throughout these exchanges Susanna Phillips had been d'Arblay's closest confidante. He and Narbonne were now meeting daily at her house for dinner. The *ménagèreship* was proving a great success – Susanna thought her guests the best and most delightful this world could provide. She did not know how long the arrangement would last. Financial clouds were gathering over her family's head; her husband was threatening to give up the cottage and retire to Ireland, where he still had some unmortgaged property. Fanny Burney, in old age, would destroy all Susanna's letters relating to her marriage and her financial troubles, so it is only from hints here and there that it is possible to gather what was happening. But one of Susanna's greatest sadnesses at this period was to be able to offer no financial help to her sister. Her own worries already seemed insoluble and the smiling exterior she presented to her guests, the pretty cottage, the charming children, were a screen for growing unhappiness.

Fanny Burney's affairs were an absorbing distraction, endlessly talked over with d'Arblay, the Locks and at last, on d'Arblay's urging, with Narbonne. The subject came as no surprise to him. He had long been aware of d'Arblay's feelings for Fanny Burney. Privately with Madame de Staël, he had been able to smile at Fanny's prudery and exaggerated fears of being compromised. But he was much too sensitive not to understand the situation and far too fond of d'Arblay not to wish the best for him.

Walking out with Susanna Phillips through the park one evening, he expanded on his worries for them both, and Susanna, jotting down their conversation in a letter that same night, was able to record it while it was still fresh in her memory.

His first view, she wrote, was all of alarm:

'If d'Arblay had even £300 income I would regard him as a being to be envied at this moment . . . But he has nothing – his greatest advantages are to have deserved the title of a distinguished French officer and to have had the confidence and friendship of M. de Lafayette – How would the Queen – how would the King look on such a choice – and then – to add to that d'Arblay has been MY FRIEND – the friend of a certain M: de Narbonne, *ci-devant* Minister of War in France – which can only add to his offences. Sadly my friendship can do nothing for him at this moment – I had hoped to have some funds I could have shared with him – I have not been able to obtain them – It would have been the greatest happiness for me – But it is useless to think of it any longer.'

Narbonne's great hope of raising money on his wife's estates in Saint Domingue had been dashed by slave uprisings and the total confusion of the situation there. It was a subject Madame de Staël would return to more than once as she tried to estimate their joint finances.

There was no need to spell this out to Susanna as they walked through the park, perhaps pacing the great yew avenue – the Druids Grove – for which Norbury was famous. It was her sister's welfare even more than d'Arblay's that he had in mind, and the worldly consequences the marriage would entail for her:

'Miss Burney, who thanks to her talents and her virtues has enjoyed the greatest success and universal approbation, has never experienced poverty – how will she, with her delicate character and health, be able to bear a life which d'Arblay, with all his strength, can only just endure – for *enfin* – even if the pension remains they'll have to live like peasants! – And the world, and the public and the general gossip – How will Miss Burney put up with the attacks which will be made on her – She who is so timid – who didn't even dare allow herself the pleasure of seeing and talking with Madame de Staël – how will she feel when she finds herself the subject of a thousand impertinences, a thousand pleasantries – won't they be death to her – won't they disgust her and distance her from her husband?'

'Never!' said Susanna, through it was hard not to be shaken by his arguments and the obvious good will which prompted them. But

94

d'Arblay, meanwhile, had been to see the Locks and their reaction had been far more sanguine, Mr Lock reiterating his belief that they could live – as many a curate did – on £120 a year. (Money would be very tight nonetheless. Eighteen years later, in *Sense and Sensibility*, neither Elinor Dashwood nor Edward Ferrars was 'quite enough in love to think that £350 a year would supply them with the comforts of life' – even allowing for wartime inflation Fanny Burney and d'Arblay would be living on much less.)

D'Arblay had returned from seeing the Locks looking 'elated and cheerful', reported Susanna, only to be cast into the depths of gloom a little later when Narbonne, in a further conversation, raised the question of a child. Fanny was forty but the possibility could not be ruled out. What prospects would it have for the future if its parents died?

'For three hours,' wrote d'Arblay to Fanny Burney, 'I was the unhappiest man on earth – for it was only at the end of that time that Mrs Phillips recalled to me that even at the very worst the child would not be reduced to beggary since it would have the money that will come to you [at Dr Burney's death]. I have only been able to breathe since then.'

With no family in England, it was to Narbonne that d'Arblay turned to speak for him in a last discussion with the Locks.

'Tomorrow,' he continued, 'M. de Narbonne will be seeing Mr Lock. I owe this mark of confidence to the man whom I love and admire the more I know him. I do not forget that in uniting myself to you I will be separating myself from him for ever. If this is the only sacrifice that I can offer you it is at least no small one.'

Narbonne's interview with Lock was evidently satisfactory for he called on Mrs Phillips immediately afterwards with a 'chearful and softened countenance' to tell her that his feelings were now entirely changed. Early that morning he had received a four-page letter from d'Arblay telling him that the matter was now decided, that his whole happiness depended on his marrying Fanny Burney. His talk with Lock had completed his conversion. 'The only thing that now concerns me,' he told her, 'is to find the best means of arriving at his goal.'

All Fanny Burney's wishes were now to be at Norbury Park, where the Locks had been urging her to stay, close to her lover and her sister. But Madame de Staël, even after her departure, could still cast a shadow over her plans. One of Dumouriez's staff officers, General Valence, who had defected to Austria with Dumouriez, was now in England, and Madame de Staël with her usual expansive good nature had invited him to stay at Juniper Hall. Narbonne could not refuse him; good manners insisted that d'Arblay too should be there to greet him, though he was in despair at the prospect. Politically well to the left of both Narbonne and d'Arblay, Valence was already under orders to leave the country; *The Times* described him as 'a member of the regicide faction in France'. Fanny was in an agony lest the newspapers should get wind of his visit to Juniper Hall, thus blackening the reputation of his hosts. At a time when it was all-important to avoid the disapproval of the royal family, it was hard to imagine a more embarrassing guest.

She had returned to London from Chessington, however, for the King's birthday reception at Buckingham House, and had been greeted, she wrote, very graciously by both King and Queen. 'They are all gone to Windsor for the Summer – & know I am going to Norbury Park – and *approve* – as M^e S [de Staël] is gone! – I was obliged to name Chesington, & its reason! – & it was most well received.'

To the intense relief of all concerned Valence's visit to Juniper Hall was not reported. Fanny breathed again and made her preparations to go to Surrey, glad to leave London where her father's meaningful silences and conscious reserve showed all too clearly what he felt about her friendship with a Frenchman and a constitutionalist. His disapproval was a further hurdle to be overcome; in the meantime, with so many doubts resolved and the backing of the Locks and her sister to cheer her, she set out for Norbury Park with a lighter heart than she had had for many weeks.

Chapter 13

Fanny Burney's letters to d'Arblay and her sister, through which it has been possible to follow their courtship so closely, not surprisingly draw to a close with her arrival at Norbury Park and the chance of seeing them both daily. The die was cast for d'Arblay. In choosing to stay in England with Fanny he had given up the chance of following Narbonne to Switzerland. It was, as he had told her, the only sacrifice he could make for her. But he was saddened at the thought of parting. Their friendship had been a rock of certainty at a time when all their world was being overturned. He admired Narbonne intensely, with something approaching hero-worship, and understood him perhaps better than anyone else. Madame de Staël, who was inclined to be dismissive of d'Arblay, had nonetheless turned to him at the time of her arrival in England to seek his help in rousing Narbonne from his depression. She would turn to him again when she felt her lover's affections might be slipping from her.

Meanwhile, as she made her way across Europe, her letters were full of nostalgia for their time together:

'I only speak English, I adore England, I cannot imagine how I could ever have said anything against it. The Rhine which recalls the Thames made me shed tears and my heart which, as you know, is filled with regrets, sees nothing but Juniper and Jenkinson's woods, all those places where I passed those four months of happiness of which I will dream until your return.'

At the same time, as she travelled away from her lover, she was preparing the ground for her long-suffering husband. Their rendez-vous was to be in Basle.

'This is an abominable journey for fatigue and inconvenience,' she wrote to him from Frankfurt. 'I hope you will receive me well after all my pains . . . I shall be very happy to see you again if it proves the beginning of a durable reunion, that is to say, of mutual happiness, for it is only on that condition that I desire and hope for it.'

It was not in Madame de Staël's nature to dissemble, or rather she could say, quite sincerely, different things to different people at the same time. She genuinely wished for a reconciliation with her husband. The experience of England had shown her how difficult it was to confront the world alone. Access to her children, a continuing income from her parents, her social position in Switzerland, all to some extent depended on his good will. Given the social conditions of the time, she had little alternative but to compromise with him as best she could.

But she could not conceal her disgust from Narbonne, especially when she learned that her husband was bringing her more debts than money:

'You know, or you do not know, that I only sought a rapprochement with him in order to be richer . . . This man adds to all his faults an extravagance and disorder impossible to imagine. He has to have his own bed to travel with, the most beautiful horses, a pack of dogs, three *valets de chambre* and with all this he's as democratic as Robespierre!'

She was able to report with satisfaction nonetheless that her husband was more in love with her than ever when they finally met on 10 June. 'I think I'll be able to get him to do what I want, but is that what I really want? An eternal third between us, instead of Juniper, of that sweet and delicious freedom of existence?' But the advantages of keeping in with him could not be disregarded, and before long she had managed to persuade him to accept Narbonne as a brother should he come to Switzerland. 'If he's able to look at you in the same way that he speaks of you he'll be an angel,' she wrote, 'but that still doesn't mean I'm enchanted by his conversation.'

The political changes in France, the expulsion of the Girondins from the National Convention, together with the royalist uprisings in the Vendée, seemed to her to offer Narbonne a new chance to come forward as a political figure and leader of moderate opinion.

'You are highly thought of here,' she told him. 'People say that the moment of your dismissal was when things began to go wrong.' Now was the time, she thought, for him to make a declaration of his political principles, explaining the events which had led up to 10 August and the deposition of the King with special relevance to his period as Minister of War, explaining too how anyone remaining loyal to the crown could not have accepted the republic. The departure of these loyalists, when the situation in France made it impossible for them to remain there, bore no relation to the departure of those émigrés who, leaving earlier, had supported the army of the Princes in fighting against France.

'Get d'Arblay to collect the material. I will write something on my side but such is your laziness that you'd use everything I've written, instead of just choosing from it, if you hadn't written your own version first.'

Her high-handed mood subsided as the days slipped past without a word from Narbonne. At home the air was thick with mute reproach and disapproval. Her mother, to underline her feelings about her daughter's wayward conduct, was in the midst of composing an essay on divorce. Ostensibly it was a response to the legislation of divorce by the National Convention eight months earlier, but in its hymn to the virtues of monogamy she was striking a blow at Madame de Staël. Necker, far milder in his attitude but torn between the imperious personalities of his wife and daughter, had his own troubles. His ill-timed pamphlet in defence of Louis XVI, as his daughter had feared, had led to the confiscation of all his possessions in France; only a few days before her arrival the seals had been set on the doors of his two houses and his name inscribed on the list of proscribed émigrés.

At any other time Madame de Staël would have been shattered by the partial ruin – for he still had property in Switzerland – of her father. But with more than three weeks gone by since her departure from England, her thoughts were focussed on only one thing – the absence of letters from her lover.

Despairingly she wrote to d'Arblay:

'My dear d'Arblay, I know you sympathize with those who are unhappy and understand better than anyone, in the midst of your own troubles, how to console others. You know to what excess I love your friend. Since I left Dover, since 10 o'clock on the night of 25 May, I have not received a single line from him. My God! is he ill? You would have written; he cannot be as ill as this frightful silence makes me fear. If he were I do not think I could survive . . . You'll think me mad but you know what an angel in heaven your friend is, you'll help me in the midst of the most violent anguish I have ever felt . . . Ah! send him to me quickly! You can, whilst regretting him, exist without him; while I through this last month have been suffering a kind of death.'

As if to make her point she collapsed a few days later with a violent inflammation of the throat. Whilst her doctor declared he had never seen a worse fever, her mother insisted there was nothing wrong with her, at the same time warning her father to avoid her for fear of catching the infection. Her husband, on the other hand, was 'sublime in his attentions'; he failed to understand, however, that all the lemonade in the world could not raise him to the level of her heart.

She was convalescing when at last a letter from Narbonne arrived. With spirits instantly restored, she was able to renew her plans for his arrival, to discuss the details of the journey, the necessity of sending his linen on ahead, the financial arrangements to be made. She was searching for a house in the canton of Geneva for the beginning of September where Talleyrand too, she hoped, would be accepted by the authorities and where Mathieu de Montmorency would be joining her. Narbonne should set out from England by August at the latest.

Narbonne sent his linen on to Switzerland but otherwise showed no eagerness to move. Without his mistress's dynamic personality to rouse him, he had sunk back into the state of melancholy and depression in which she had found him when she first joined him in England. The projected declaration of his principles remained unwritten, nor did Madame de Staël proceed with her own draft for it. A more immediate subject claimed her attention, the fate of the luckless Marie Antoinette. Imprisoned in the Temple, but soon to be separated from her children and taken to the Conciergerie, she had become the focus of all the anti-royalist hatreds of the French. The Austrian 'she wolf' was a figure of infamy, accused of every kind of sexual vice, regarded as a traitor who had sought to plot the ruin of the Revolution. In the mood induced by the Terror it was obvious that her trial and execution would not be long in coming.

Madame de Staël had never been a favourite of the Queen, who detested both her politics and her noisy intriguing on behalf of her father and Narbonne. She might well accept the argument, as her royalist supporters did, that it had been the constitutionalists who had opened the way to all her subsequent misfortunes. But Madame de Staël, as Talleyrand once put it drily, was always ready to throw her friends into the water in order to fish them out again. Now she flung all her energies into composing a pamphlet in defence of the Queen, just as her father had done for Louis XVI. Two editions would be printed, one in Geneva and one in London, where Talleyrand supervised the proofs and publication. They were naturally condemned in France, where such pamphlets as were found were confiscated.

In defending the Queen, Madame de Staël paid little attention to the political ups and downs of the past. The main thrust of her pamphlet was an appeal for sympathy with the Queen as a widow, as a wife and mother, whose fate should touch the hearts of every woman whatever their political convictions. The pamphlet may have deserved criticism – it was, said a Swiss neighbour, Madame de Charrière, a mass of false sentiment and disingenuousness. But there was no doubting the courage that lay behind it. By writing it she was cutting herself off from Paris definitively, and reducing any hopes she might have that her father's fortune could yet be saved. She was also, though this she took more lightly, making her husband's position still more difficult should he be posted back in Paris as ambassador.

She never had the slightest hesitation, however, about the rightness of what she was doing, nor did she allow considerations of expediency to prevent her from doing her utmost to save other victims of the Terror, which now held France in its grip. Her house in

Switzerland would certainly be a haven for Narbonne, but it was a haven too for friends escaping from the guillotine. Over the next few months she would devote her energies to mounting an elaborate rescue operation for friends and even strangers in danger of their lives. Her husband's diplomatic status made it possible for her to provide false papers on arrival; lavish bribes, and the same exertion of charm and emotional blackmail which she had expended on Narbonne's rescuer Dr Bollman, bought her the services of agents who would venture into France to bring back those in trouble. Their method was simple: the holder of a Swiss passport, with an appearance roughly matching that of the person to be rescued, would travel to meet them in Paris and hand over his (or her) papers. The rescued person would cross into Switzerland by a different frontier post, while the original passport-holder, returning by his previous route, would claim that he had lost his papers on the way, and if necessary call on the local magistrate to confirm his identity. The escaper, more often than not, would end up under the roof of Madame de Staël, where he would use a borrowed Swedish name to avoid embarrassment with the Swiss authorities who did not wish for trouble with France.

In the midst of these activities Narbonne, according to her letters, remained her chief preoccupation. It was only in the thought of their reunion, she wrote, that she could tear her mind from the bloodshed that was going on elsewhere:

'Death is the only government in France; the soul succumbs beneath such horrors. Next to you all is enchantment, my imagination is only occupied in contemplating you, my heart in loving you, but here, without you, my thoughts range over the horrible spectacles which I see each day in the news.'

From Juniper Hall, deprived of all hope of helping friends and relatives in danger, the view must have looked still more despairing. D'Arblay had had no news of his family since he had left France with Lafayette. His parents were dead, but his only brother had been an ardent royalist; it seemed unlikely he would survive the purge of so-called aristocrats and traitors taking place in France. Narbonne's youngest daughter was still a hostage to fortune; three months later, when the Terror was at its height, Madame de Staël would arrange for her to be brought to safety in the Swedish embassy. Meanwhile, perhaps, it was the thought of her that made him make a special favourite of Mrs Phillips's daughter Fanny; the eight-year-old Norbury, on the other hand, regarded d'Arblay as his 'intimatest friend'.

Facing an unknown future, with poverty and privation as an immediate prospect, there was nothing to do, as Talleyrand put it, but exist, while awaiting a counter-revolution in France that would fit in with their aims. A royalist reaction in France would suit them not much better than the Jacobin régime. Patriots as they were, the spectacle of their country's sufferings was a harrowing one, their one ray of hope and pride the achievements of the French army, welded into a national force as never before by opposition from without. It had been impossible not to rejoice at the earlier French victories of Jemappes and Valmy; even now, with England participating in the war, their feelings remained ambiguous. But the Terror, and the police state it implied, were the internal means of enforcing unity. However much they might wish France to succeed against the dangers of invasion, they could not look on the conflicts which were tearing the country apart with anything but horror. The death of the Queen, as a symbol of France's defiance of the allied powers, would give the final twist to the pattern of their divided loyalties.

Chapter 14

On 23 July, in a letter to Narbonne, Madame de Staël made a casual reference to an interesting new figure who had appeared in Switzerland. It was the Swedish Count Ribbing, notorious as one of those who had planned the assassination of the Swedish King Gustavus III fifteen months earlier at the famous masked ball immortalized later in Verdi's *Un Ballo in Maschera*. The chief assassin, Count Ankarström, had been executed; Ribbing, as one of the co-conspirators, had been sentenced to death but later pardoned and sent into exile. He was travelling in Europe under the pseudonym of Bing, but his assumed name was no more than a sop to local authorities; his reputation and his dangerous glamour as a republican who had risked his life in what he felt to be a righteous cause made him immediately attractive to Madame de Staël.

To Narbonne she treated her new acquaintance lightly:

'There is here, under an assumed name, a certain Cte Ribbing, the famous accomplice of Anckarström. We do not see him; all the same, under different pretexts he has twice met us while we were out walking. His face is superb for those who like what is called beauty . . . For the rest he seems to have a great desire to fall in love with me but as long as M. de Staël is here his position of ambassador to Sweden makes it impossible for me to see him.'

It was a fleeting mention in a letter filled with longing for her lover's presence. Narbonne, she wrote, was her sole source of happiness, the greatest to be found in this life and perhaps in heaven too. 'I love that remark of Mrs Lock: "I hope I don't offend the divinity in believing that his paradise could not surpass my own." Ah! come here and I will believe it.' All the same, despite her protestations and her husband's position, she was beginning to see the handsome young regicide. Two years later, looking back on a stormy liaison, she described their love as dating from the July of 1793.

In England Narbonne kept his own counsel as the passionate letters from his mistress poured in. He did not discuss her with d'Arblay, who was in any case absorbed in his own worries. Talleyrand, ostensibly a boon companion, was a dangerous ally where Madame de Staël was concerned. He may not have taken his affair with her very seriously – 'there was absolute confusion in such matters,' he said later – but observers in Paris had noted signs of jealousy when she turned her attentions to Narbonne. He would later repay her friendship with cool ingratitude, disclaiming her when she was out of favour with Napoleon. He would serve Narbonne no better, when in his years as Foreign Minister he did nothing to further his friend's career. 'Narbonne has nothing and needs nothing,' he maintained airily. 'He has his books and his friends . . . there is no need to worry about him.' Later, when Talleyrand had been disgraced and Narbonne became his aide de camp, Napoleon said to him: 'How is it that Talleyrand, your great friend who knew you better than anyone, always persuaded me against employing you? I think at heart he was afraid of you.'

These were betrayals still far in the future. But Madame de Staël had her own ways of playing her friends against each other, keeping up a correspondence with Talleyrand and complaining to Narbonne when she felt she was being neglected. 'Why hasn't the bishop written to me,' she asked him anxiously; later when Narbonne in his turn seemed insufficiently attentive, she began to suspect that Talleyrand was plotting against her with her lover. She would explore the complexities of their relationship in her novel *Delphine*, where the character of Talleyrand is transposed to that of Madame

Vernon who, behind a mask of subtle and caressing charm, cold-heartedly schemes to detach the heroine from her lover. It was apropos of this transposed portrait that Talleyrand would make his famous *bon mot*: 'I hear you have written a novel in which both you and I appear as women.'

Such complex relationships were beyond the reach of the straight-forward d'Arblay. His loyalty to Narbonne was absolute, all other permutations secondary. It was to d'Arblay that Narbonne, when he finally left England, would entrust the letters he had received from Madame de Staël – perhaps he felt it would be unsafe to carry them with him in case he was arrested on his journey across Europe; perhaps he simply wished to leave them behind, the passionate torrent of alternating love and reproaches having operated finally on the law of diminishing returns. They would be found a hundred and fifty years later, bundled up amongst the Burney papers, with Fanny Burney's prim notation:'*Lettres brûlantes à brûler* – a fine moral lesson too.'

July 1793 was a dramatic month in France. Civil war was raging in the Vendée, the Girondins were trying unsuccessfully to rally their forces in the provinces and Charlotte Corday, despairing of their resolve, assassinated Marat in his bath. Madame de Staël wondered at her courage, and sent an account of her execution from a Paris correspondent to Narbonne. Fanny Burney, now installed at Norbury Park, paid little notice to what was going on across the Channel. Her thoughts were almost wholly taken up with her approaching marriage and the last great obstacle to be overcome, her father's total disapproval of the project.

Fanny loved her father dearly – only Mr Lock and now her suitor d'Arblay were worthy to be compared with him, in her opinion. He had rejoiced at her success when *Evelina* made her a celebrity and he himself was basking in the fame of his *History of Music*. Together they had gone out into society, comparing notes of their triumphs and encounters with the great. Fanny's entry into the royal service, which had promised so much, had proved a woeful disappointment, but it had certainly enhanced her social standing. To see her throw it all away on a penniless French émigré, whose politics could only be displeasing to the Court, and would close most Tory doors against her too, was a prospect that filled him with dismay.

'Dear Fanny,' he wrote to her pathetically, 'I have for some time seen very plainly that you were *éprise*. You must have observed my silent gravity surpassing that of mere illness and its consequent low spirits. I had some thoughts of writing to Susan about it, and intended begging her to do what I must now do for myself – that is, beg, warn and admonish you not to entangle yourself in a wild and romantic attachment which offers nothing in prospect but poverty and distress.'

But Fanny was long past pleas or admonitions; the only question now was one of tactics. The Locks, her confidants throughout the courtship, were asked to write to Dr Burney supporting d'Arblay in his request for Fanny's hand. Such formalities were more suited to someone in their twenties than their forties, but Fanny had always played the role of docile daughter and she was not going to step out of it now.

D'Arblay's letter was short and fervent as he declared his intention of devoting his life to Fanny's happiness and his respect and admiration for her father. Mr Lock's was longer and more practical. From all he had seen and learnt of d'Arblay's character he was convinced that he would make Fanny as 'happy as good sense, delicate feelings and sound principles may be expected to make a woman so peculiarly formed to be affected by them'.

'Their circumstances,' he added, 'will indeed be narrow; but his plan of life is proportioned to them & I never met a man who seemed, from the paucity of his personal wants, better calculated to render everything beyond the purely personal superfluous.'

Dr Burney was not convinced.

'My children,' he wrote with dignity to Lock, 'have no other right to the addresses of persons of fortune than the want of it themselves. All the self-denying virtues of Epictetus will not keep off indigence in a state of society without the assistance of patrimony, profession or possessions . . . on one side or the other.'

To d'Arblay he wrote in similar terms, suggesting a postponement to the marriage till the situation in France had changed or he had found some kind of occupation.

'A person of your abilities and habits of life,' he told him, 'has a right to aspire to something better than obscurity and a cottage. Affection dissipates every cloud of difficulty in Theory . . . but as the school of adversity will be new to you both I very much fear its effects will be more irksome in participation, than to either of you singly.'

To such apparently just and reasonable arguments it was hard to find an answer. But Susanna Phillips, ever zealous in her sister's interests, came to the rescue with a letter still further pleading their cause, setting out their plans and means minutely, 'clearly demonstrating their power of Happiness, with willing œconomy, congenial tastes and mutual love of the Country'. Dr Burney had always found Susanna hard to resist; at the same time d'Arblay's most distinguished friends in England, the Prince de Poix and the Marquis de Lally Tollendal, wrote to him with warm recommendations of d'Arblay's character, integrity and record of distinguished service. A fortnight after d'Arblay's first request, 'in trembling even to reluctance', he sent his cold consent to their marriage, though refusing to give his daughter away or be present at the wedding ceremony.

The way was now open to their marriage, though such was the tone of Dr Burney's letter that on his second reading of it d'Arblay gave way to momentary despair. Had he really the right to involve Fanny in his poverty and misfortune? Would not the world think that she had committed a folly and he had behaved unworthily in demanding such a sacrifice?

For a courtship that had depended so much on letters, it was right that Fanny's reply should be in writing:

'Whether to share your fate or not no longer depends on me. I know well that I would follow you everywhere . . . I am yours for life, come what may, my dear – noble – more, more than ever dear and estimable friend.'

Her note was in French, d'Arblay's written on the same page, in French also:

'I receive your sweet assurances with rapture. I have nothing to add to what I have already said, my first words were the deepest wishes of my heart and the engagement of my whole life. It is for you alone to dispose of it.'

This exchange, as Fanny noted, completed the previous correspondence between them: 'In a very short time after my hand followed my heart.'

Fanny's wedding to d'Arblay took place on 28 July in the little Norman church at Mickleham. In the absence of her father her eldest brother James gave her away. Mr Lock was d'Arblay's best man; Narbonne, Mrs Lock and the Phillipses were the only other guests. Two days later the ceremony was completed according to Roman Catholic rites in the chapel of the Sardinian embassy in London. 'And NEVER – NEVER,' wrote Fanny, 'was union more exquisitely blessed and felicitous – though, after the first 8 years of unmingled happiness, it was assailed by many calamities – chiefly of separation or illness – Yet still mentally unbroken.'

The newly married couple took rooms in a farmhouse close to Mickleham. Mr Lock had given them a piece of land in Norbury Park on which they later planned to build a house. Meanwhile Fanny's first preoccupation was to break the news of her marriage to the Queen through her Lady in Waiting, Mrs de Luc. It was with intense relief that she received a letter from Mrs Schwellenberg, her old colleague at Court, ten days later, conveying the congratulations of the Queen and all the royal family. A further letter shortly after from another member of the royal household showed how well her husband's case was understood: 'It is with the Wretches of France we are at war – nothing could be more unjust than to extend our prejudices against their victims.'

The pension which had caused her so much anxiety was safe, and if there were sneers in the newspapers and outspoken disapproval from friends such as Mrs Ord and Mr Hutton, there were enough whole-hearted congratulations from those who loved her to make her cup of happiness full. Congratulations came in from d'Arblay's friends, from Talleyrand who declared that her novels had repaid him for the pains of exile, from Madame de Staël, warm-hearted as ever and incapable of bearing grudges.

'Now that you've become in some way part of my family,' she wrote, 'I hope that if I return to England I shall see you as often as I like, that is constantly. All my regrets and all my hopes are still in Surrey. It is an earthly paradise to me; it will be so to you I hope. I know no one with a better character to live with than

M. d'Arblay, and I've known for a long time how much he loves you.'

Fanny did not share the ambassadress's wish to meet again; even now, with the royal family's approval in her pocket, Madame de Staël was a dangerous friend to be associated with. But she continued to admire her talents and to delight in her works over the years. Madame de Staël, on the other hand, would declare with some truth that once she got married Fanny Burney never wrote so well again.

Chapter 15

Narbonne stayed on a few weeks longer at Juniper Hall. But the lease was coming to an end, and he no longer had the means to renew it, arranging instead to stay on in Mickleham with the Phillipses as a paying guest. He moved out of the house at the beginning of September and new tenants, the royal family's doctor, Sir Lucas Pepys and his family, took over. The new Madame d'Arblay remembered him well from her days at Court and reported with satisfaction to her father that they had made their first call in the neighbourhood on her.

Soon after their marriage the d'Arblays had moved from the rooms they had taken to the greater privacy of a cottage near Bookham, about two miles from Mickleham. Narbonne, with Talleyrand and Beaumetz, who were enjoying a last few days of hospitality at Juniper Hall, came to see them in their new abode and Susanna hastened to repeat their comments to her sister:

'Our Messieurs are delighted wth you – M. de Talleyrand – "Her pretty face – with happiness written on it" M. de Beaumetz – "And her beautiful eyes" – M. de Talleyrand "and how she knows how to use them" – M. de Narbonne "and how she listens with her eyes . . ." etc.etc. I can't think why I'm repeating all this, it gives me infinite distress!'

Dr Burney, despite his resistance to the marriage, was much too fond of his daughter to continue aloof. Before long they were exchanging letters as of old, with presents of books for d'Arblay who, as Fanny said, could never stir without a book in his pocket or his hand. Returning from a visit to Chelsea College, d'Arblay took over the dining-room table to arrange his tiny library – 'No great mischief,' said Fanny cheerfully, 'for he can far better *cover* it than our cook.' Even in their straitened circumstances there was no question of not having a servant, scarcely an extravagance when a cook could be hired for £5 a year.

The summer months passed happily for the newly-married couple. On most days when the weather was fine they would walk across the fields to see the Locks or Mrs Phillips, d'Arblay carrying a folding chair so that Fanny could rest on the way. At home d'Arblay had developed a passion for gardening. Having never held a spade before, he now dug for hours in the two-acre plot behind the cottage, using his army sabre to cut down the most luxuriant weeds or trim the hedge. Fanny meanwhile was working on a new novel, *Camilla*, which they hoped would do much to better their fortunes. (Two years later they were able to build a house, Camilla Cottage, with the proceeds from the novel.)

Newspapers were expensive and the d'Arblays relied on seeing the news when they visited Norbury Park. In early August the British army under the Duke of York was humiliatingly defeated at Dunkirk. But at the end of the same month the British navy under Admiral Hood achieved a brilliant coup when the French port of Toulon, which they had been blockading, came over to the allied cause. Louis XVII, the ten-year-old former Dauphin, now imprisoned in the Temple, was proclaimed King. For a moment it seemed as though Toulon might provide the starting point for a counter-revolution which would spread through the disaffected south and west of France.

To the constitutionalists, chafing impotently in England, the possibilities seemed as great as they had been at the time of Dumouriez's attempted coup. It was a complex situation. A monarchy had been proclaimed but it was not clear whether it was to be a constitutional one or the old absolutist variety the royalist émigrés desired. At first things seemed hopeful when Hood, in a proclamation from Toulon, promised support for a monarchy on the lines of the constitution of 1791, to which the constitutionalists had pledged their loyalty. Inspired by Hood's proclamation, and feeling honour-bound to support it, D'Arblay wrote to Pitt, offering his services as a soldier in any expedition planned for Toulon. Narbonne and Talleyrand scented greater prizes, nothing less than the establishment of a constitutionalist government in France should the risings in the south succeed.

'The constitutionalists,' wrote Talleyrand to Madame de Staël, 'are the only ones who can hope to do and undo things . . . the constitution is the only way to rally people's spirits.'

He envisaged a gathering of all the former deputies of the Constituent Assembly at Toulon, with an inner executive including Narbonne as Minister of War. If Lyons, at present besieged by the troops of the National Convention, succeeded in defeating them, they would be well on the way to a successful counter-revolution backed by Britain and the other allied powers.

'You who love proclamations,' he told Madame de Staël, 'have you thought of all that could be done in this respect? But don't send anything about this to Narbonne. In our present situation we need to act on a day-to-day basis. Don't tempt his vanity by sending him something already written.'

Fanny d'Arblay had been heartbroken at her husband's offer to go to Toulon. She had hoped he had given up the 'profession of blood' for ever when he married her. But she gave her reluctant consent to his initiative, knowing that where he felt his honour was involved, she had no right to stop him. Fortunately for her, however, Pitt did not support Hood's declaration. He had no desire to be committed to a specifically constitutionalist solution – the royalist émigrés in any case were far more numerous and powerful. D'Arblay's offer was refused; like his fellow constitutionalists, he was relegated to the sidelines.

Meanwhile, things were going badly at Toulon. Reinforcements from Britain's allies failed to materialize, or when they did were wholly inadequate. The fall of Lyons, amidst terrible reprisals, released new French troops to surround Toulon; the British attackers were forced to become defenders. A second British fleet sent to reinforce Hood's ships was beaten off by French artillery. By early November Talleyrand admitted ruefully that the affair of Toulon was finished for the constitutionalists. In December, thanks largely to the skill of a young artillery captain, Napoleon Bonaparte, Toulon fell to the French republic, leaving the royalist émigrés as bitterly disappointed as their constitutionalist counterparts.

Madame de Staël had never had great hopes of Toulon, believing rightly that the French would never surrender to an outside power and that their salvation could only come from within. Meanwhile the news from France elsewhere was frightful. On 16 October Marie Antoinette went to the scaffold, to be followed three weeks later by twenty-one leading Girondins. Terror had been proclaimed the order of the day; every week brought fresh news of executions and arrests. In late October, using the services of a trusted messenger who sought them out in France, she was able to rescue two of her dearest friends.

'With difficulties almost incredible,' wrote Fanny Burney to her father, 'Me de Staël has contrived, a second time, to save the lives of M. de Jaucourt & M. de Montmorenci, who are just arrived in Switzerland. We know as yet none of the particulars: simply that they are saved is all; but they write in a style the most melancholy to M. de Narbonne, of the dreadful fanaticism of License, which they dare call Liberty, that still reigns unsubdued in France. And they have preserved nothing but their persons! – of their vast properties they could secure no more than pocket money, for travelling in the most penurious manner. They are therefore in a state the most deplorable. Switzerland is filled with Gentlemen and Ladies of the very first families and rank, who are all starving, but those who have had the *good fortune* to procure, by disguising their quality, some menial office!'

With Madame de Staël and her husband, in a house she had just rented near Nyon, Jaucourt and Montmorency were at least spared the worst misfortunes of their fellow countrymen. But they found their hostess in a dreadful state. Narbonne, who had been expected in September, still showed no sign of arriving. His excuse was that his interests in the West Indies, with the British on the verge of invading the island of Saint Domingue, demanded his presence in England. He owed it to his wife and children to save what property he could. Madame de Staël was indignant. Had he not two sons in Switzerland with claims as strong as theirs? Did he owe nothing to the woman who had risked her life in saving his? She suspected a deeper motive for his absence. It was Talleyrand, she declared, who had schemed to set him against her; she had feared as much when she left England. Her reproaches rose in a crescendo:

'Believe me M. de Narbonne, you make me suffer too much. Whatever depths of depravity the company of the bishop, that man who treats life and death as a game, has led you to, when you are told that my blood is streaming over the face of my unhappy child, that this knife, my last remaining comfort, has found the heart which can no longer live without you, you will shudder more than you imagine . . . When you see in yourself the assassin of everything that loved you, even your fickle nature will not save you from remorse.'

The idea that Narbonne might join an expedition to Toulon renewed her suspicions of Talleyrand's influence and her threats of suicide:

'If you go to Toulon I shall kill myself . . . I shall go to Paris and assassinate Robespierre and help you by expiring.'

It was Talleyrand, she insisted, who had seduced him with his treacherous advice; by himself he would never have dealt her such a devastating blow. But she kept her furies for her letters to Narbonne, and continued to write to Talleyrand with plans for his arrival in Switzerland.

Narbonne, over their long relationship, must have learned to discount her most dramatic statements, which owed much to the style of eighteenth-century tragedy, still more to current horrors in France. But even without the pangs of unrequited love with which she reproached him, his absence put her in a humiliating position in the eyes of her parents and her Swiss neighbours. They had seen her leave for England against all persuasions to follow her lover, abandoning her children and her long-suffering husband. Her mother had constantly warned her that Narbonne would be unfaithful; his past of extravagance and love affairs revealed it all too clearly. Now, on her return to Switzerland, with a house made ready for her lover, with the local authorities prepared to accept his presence, he was showing no eagerness to join her and the world was a witness to his lack of concern.

Surprisingly, it was her husband who seemed most sympathetic. Finding her in a state of prostration one day, he promised to escort her to Frankfurt whence she could travel on to England should Narbonne persist in his excuses not to join her. 'I know that I will lose my credit in France and thus in Sweden,' he told her, 'but your life is more precious to me than anything and I can see that you are dying.'

It was one of Madame de Staël's misfortunes that she could not love her husband, however much he seemed to be in love with her. His greatest fault, and the least easy to forgive, was that he bored her, that the life of activity and intellectual excitement she needed meant nothing to him.

'You don't like my friends,' she told him, 'and I cannot exist without them. Intelligent and animated conversation is not essential to you; I go to sleep without it. You can exist peacefully in the Swiss countryside; I think the grave is preferable.'

She was touched, however, by his self-sacrificing offer. But though she wrote to Mrs Phillips announcing her arrival in England and to Narbonne asking him to find her a smaller house than Juniper Hall where there would be room for their elder son, Auguste, her heart was never really in the project. Despite her anguished complaints to Narbonne she was seeing more of the young Count Ribbing, who in his turn showed signs of falling in love with her. More importantly still, in Switzerland she could shelter the friends she had saved and continue saving others. During the months of the Terror she rescued more than twenty people, among them Mathieu de Montmorency's mother and Jaucourt's beloved Madame de la Châtre. She was not always successful; it fell to her to break the news to Mathieu de Montmorency that his brother had died on the scaffold. Every week brought news of others who had perished.

Looking back on that period one of the things which she remembered most, in long walks beside Lake Geneva, was the contrast between the calm and peace of nature with the horrors unloosed by man across the water. 'Her talent maintained a religious silence,' wrote Sainte-Beuve in a famous passage, 'while from far off were heard, muffled and thick as the beating of oars upon the lake, the measured strokes of the guillotine upon the scaffold.'

Chapter 16

The defeat of the British at Toulon and the growing successes of the French elsewhere had created repercussions back in England, redoubling the government's determination to pursue the war on ideological as well as practical grounds. Jacobinism was the enemy; harsh sentences were passed on those found guilty of sedition and in the treason trials that autumn the defendants, Horne Tooke and others, would have faced the death sentence had they not been acquitted. Fear and suspicion of the French in England were reaching hysterical proportions. Talleyrand had always been a dubious figure in official eyes; he was equally detested in the courts of Austria and Prussia. In the aftermath of Toulon, perhaps as a gesture to their allies, the government invoked the Aliens bill to order his expulsion.

'Last Tuesday, at five o'clock in the evening,' he wrote to Madame de Staël, 'two men appeared at my door, one of whom told me he was a messenger of the state and that he had come to serve an order from the King signifying that I must leave his kingdom within five days.'

News of this bombshell brought Narbonne hurrying up to London to help his friend. Whilst Talleyrand appealed against the order in letters to Pitt and Grenville, Narbonne tried his utmost to get the Duke of Gloucester to intervene with the King, and vainly sought an interview with Pitt. The most they could obtain was a delay of three weeks in order to enable him to wind up his affairs.

'Can you think of a worse misfortune?' wrote Narbonne to Mrs Phillips, ' . . . and yet with all this nothing equals his calm, his courage, almost his gaiety. Would not yours and that of our adorable friends at Norbury suffer a little if I had received a similar order? . . . Alas, I am neither more guilty nor more innocent than my unhappy friend who charges me to tell you all of his unshakeable devotion.'

Talleyrand was too well known and the news of his expulsion too public for him to make the journey across Europe to Switzerland in safety. The risk of interception by French ships made the voyage to Denmark equally dangerous. In the end he decided to seek refuge in America. His friend the Chevalier de Beaumetz, 'as simply as though he had been a brother', offered to go with him, and Talleyrand with equal simplicity accepted his offer.

There was no time to write to Madame de Staël for a transfer of money. It was Narbonne who arranged a loan for him with Mr Lock's close friend, the great financier John Julius Angerstein, against the security of his West Indian property. Since the outcome of affairs in Saint Domingue, with the slaves in revolt and the British about to invade, was far from certain, it seems that Angerstein's loan was more generous than secure.

Before embarking, Talleyrand wrote letters of farewell to his friends in Surrey. He too had been touched by Mrs Phillips's charm and sweetness and his letter thanked her for her many kindnesses:

'My thoughts will be with you, with the Captain, with your children, all my life. You are going to have a zealous servant in America; I shall not come back to Europe without visiting Surrey: everything that has some value for my mind and heart is there.'

To d'Arblay he wrote with special warmth:

'Goodbye my dear d'Arblay, I am leaving your country till it is no longer swayed by petty human passions. Then I will return; not, in truth, to occupy myself with affairs for it is a long time since I abandoned them for ever, but to see the excellent inhabitants of Surrey . . . I do not know how long I will stay in America: if something stable and reasonable can be restored in our unhappy country I will come back; if Europe is destroyed in the next campaign I shall prepare a refuge in America for all our friends. Goodbye. My homage to Madame d'Arblay and Madame Phillips. I ask and promise you friendship for life.'

Talleyrand set out for America on 2 March 1793. 'At the age of thirty-nine I am starting a new life,' he told Madame de Staël, 'for it is life that I want. I love my friends too much to have other ideas; and then I wish to proclaim, and proclaim loudly, what I have wanted, what I have done, what I have prevented, what I have regretted; I wish to show how much I have loved liberty and how much I still love it.'

'I felt a kind of contentment,' he wrote later. 'It seemed to me that in that time of almost universal misery, I would almost have regretted not being persecuted too.'

Narbonne saw his friends on to their ship, the *William Penn*, and stayed with them till the moment of embarcation. For a quarter of an hour he watched their ship sail down the Thames, then took the road back to Surrey, the only place, he told d'Arblay, where he was happy, 'surrounded by everything that is good and amiable in this world'. But he had been saddened by his friends' departure and had hardly arrived back at Mickleham before he sent another note to d'Arblay expressing a real desire and need to see him, since there was no one left but him.

Talleyrand's departure had been widely publicized, not only in the British papers but in those abroad. In one of these, *La Correspondance Politique*, it was announced that Narbonne, the former Minister of War, had also been expelled. It was a statement all too near the truth. It was only thanks to the 'inexhaustible kindness' of Mrs Phillips, as he told her, that he had been able to live away from London, thus escaping the hatreds to which Talleyrand had been exposed. But his position was far from secure. Public opinion was vociferous against the French. In Talleyrand's opinion it would not be long before all the constitutionalists were obliged to leave England.

Madame de Staël was appalled by Talleyrand's expulsion.

'It's certain then that the bishop has left for America,' she wrote to Narbonne. 'Ah, what anguish this frightful news has caused me. I can scarcely write to you my eyes are so filled with tears; and not a word from you at this terrible moment!'

Now, more than ever, it seemed to her, Narbonne should come to Switzerland, to make up for the sufferings he had caused her, to avoid the humiliation of being expelled. Her correspondence with him had grown increasingly one-sided. Narbonne's letters to her have not survived, but there are echoes of his letters in hers, his promises to leave England, his reassurances of love, finally as time went by his protests at the violence of her language and emotions. Nothing, it seemed, would stir him to departure.

'It seems that there's perhaps a lack of courage in the difficulties he makes in deciding,' Talleyrand had written to Mathieu de Montmorency. 'He stays where he is because he's there and because he fears any kind of movement in the precarious situation that he is in . . . When Narbonne does reach you, you must give him support; our situation depresses him too much; he must be taken out of himself.'

To Madame de Staël mere apathy was not a sufficient reason for Narbonne to break her heart. She accused him of falling in love with Mrs Phillips; she declared that she would come to England and throw herself at her feet. To the Locks she wrote deploring his infidelity:

'Is it near your angelic family that M. de Narbonne learns to break every tie of friendship and gratitude? He does not condescend to answer my letters and weary of repeating false promises about his arrival he finds it easier to break with a person to whom he owes more than imagination can conceive. I return without ceasing to this terrible subject, for the betrayal of a friend seems to me the poison of life and to taste of it is death.'

It is not surprising that Narbonne began to feel hunted and ridiculous. He was not a man for *grandes passions*; as an elegant product of the old régime he was accustomed to take his love affairs lightly. The extraordinary circumstances of the Revolution, their passionate involvement in its events, had bound him together with Madame de Staël in a common cause. He owed her his life and innumerable acts of thoughtfulness and generosity since. 'By what inconceivable enchantment,' he once asked her, 'are you both my divinity and my *valet de chambre*?' But already in England he had been embarrassed by the intensity of her feelings for him and her carelessness of scandal in revealing them. Once out of her orbit, the thought of leaving Surrey to be swept up once again in her tempestuous wake seemed less and less appealing.

Madame de Staël's reproaches did not cease, but she had her consolations in the growing ardour of Count Ribbing. Since her husband had left for Denmark on a diplomatic mission in early February, any embarrassment Ribbing's presence in her household might have caused was avoided. Only the devoted Mathieu de Montmorency, who had accepted her relations with Narbonne, showed signs of being irritated by this new intruder.

Madame de Staël was unabashed. Ribbing's love could be used as ammunition against Narbonne.

'You know what I told you about Ribbing,' she wrote to Narbonne. 'I've made the mistake of letting him love me to distraction ... If I thought that his incredible beauty could act on my senses, that in giving myself to him I would find five minutes of intoxication, I would do so this evening. Twenty times I've turned towards him with an effort, as though it were a duty; I've said to him "*Eh bien*, I will love you, I think I will be able to." He flings himself upon his knees, he wants to clasp me in his arms, and then the chill of death comes over me and I repeat to him with passion that you, and only you in the world, have the right to my heart.'

Such playing with fire could not go on for long. By the end of April Ribbing had become her lover, though she took pains to conceal it. Her husband and parents remained in perfect ignorance of her new attachment, and her much-discussed liaison with Narbonne provided a smokescreen for her love affair with Ribbing.

Madame de Staël had always been on the worst of terms with her mother, whose disapproval of her conduct had been a constant factor for the last five years. For some time Madame Necker's health had been bad (she was suffering from dropsy), and by the spring of 1794 it became clear that she had not long to live. Madame de Staël, somewhat reluctantly, left her friends to be by her side. Unaware of her daughter's new liaison, Madame Necker continued to reproach her for the previous one. One morning, after a crisis in the night during which she had nearly died, she called her daughter to her bedside.

'My daughter,' she told her, 'I am dying of the sorrow caused me by your guilty and public attachment; you are punished by the behaviour of its object towards you; in abandoning you he has achieved what all my prayers had failed to do. It is by your care for your father that you will obtain my pardon in heaven. Leave me, do not answer me, I have not the strength to argue at this moment.'

'I left her,' wrote Madame de Staël, 'and I did not die, since I am not dead.'

Madame Necker died on 8 June. By then the correspondence between her daughter and Narbonne had foundered into mutual recriminations. Despite repeated promises to join her Narbonne remained in England, ostensibly with his West Indian interests in mind. He was exasperated, in any case, by the way Madame de Staël proclaimed her sorrows far and wide, mingling talk of the money she had given him with her complaints of his ingratitude. Stung by her reference to Ribbing, he compared her to 'the most despicable of *filles*'. For Madame de Staël the disillusion was complete. 'I dreamed of what I was to you,' she wrote, 'and the only truth lies in my letters.'

In her essay on the passions she traced the process of her disenchantment:

'Nothing equals the despair of realizing that the object of one's love is unworthy of it. This fatal knowledge penetrates the reason before detaching the heart. Still feeling the emotion which one knows one must renounce, one loves while no longer esteeming; one behaves as though there was still hope, while suffering because there is none; one yearns towards the image one has created; one turns to those same characteristics which once seemed the emblem of virtue, only to be repulsed by what is far more cruel than hate, by the total lack of any sensibility or depth of feeling.'

Madame Récamier, Madame de Staël's great friend in later years, summed up the matter more succinctly:

'Narbonne behaved very badly to Madame de Staël, as men often do when they have been successful.'

Narbonne had spent his year in England living quietly in the country, reading much and finding his chief pleasure in the company of his neighbours and the simple hospitality of the Phillips family.

On occasional visits to London he had talked to leading members of the Whig opposition, Erskine, Sheridan and Charles James Fox, who would become a lifelong friend. But apart from his one unavailing interview at the time of Louis XVI's trial he had no contact with Pitt, who had refused to see or answer him when Talleyrand was expelled. One evening in May, however, quite unexpectedly, he was invited to dine with the Prime Minister at his country house.

He would long remember the interview with Pitt, recalling it word for word years later in conversation with his secretary and biographer, Abel François Villemain. He found Pitt, normally so calm and cold, filled with a hatred towards revolutionary France that seemed as much personal as political, and determined to win the war at whatever cost. After expressing his feelings of horror and regret at events in France, he moved towards the real object of his interview.

'You did wonders for your country before the follies and crimes of the Jacobin faction,' he told him. 'In just a few months you had built up your fortifications, re-established their garrisons, and put an army of one hundred and fifty thousand men on a war footing. But today they've nothing left but chaos and deficit . . . For the safety of Europe and civil order everywhere we must be ready for a long and implacable war till the scourge of revolution is destroyed.'

Narbonne replied by advising the Prime Minister not to embark on a war to the death with France; its only result would be to unite the country in desperate resistance, in the same way that the Duke of Brunswick's manifesto had done earlier.

'I knew you were a Whig,' said Pitt, 'you talk like Erskine in trying to discourage and discredit the war; but I know you are a good Frenchman too, as noble in character as your name.'

He went on to ask Narbonne the best means of attacking France, questioning him searchingly on France's military capabilities and resources.

'It's a question of life or death for civilization. All right-thinking men must help each other. Whether you're aristocrats or constitutionalists you have all been equally denounced, dispossessed and murdered. Your views, your least conjectures would be immensely valuable to us.'

'I detest the bloodthirsty measures of the committees of the National Convention as much as you do,' replied Narbonne. 'I can expect only death and condemnation from them. But if from my period of administration as Minister, and my memory of it, I uttered one word which was harmful to my country's military defence I should look on myself as a traitor – and I would be.'

The conversation closed soon after. The two men parted coldly. A few weeks later, as Narbonne half expected, he too was ordered to leave England.

Chapter 17

———❦———

Narbonne's farewells to his friends at Norbury were full of sadness. Until he saw his children and his mother again, he told the Locks, he would regard them as his closest family. We know nothing of his parting with Mrs Phillips, though he writes of 'a good little letter' from her three weeks later. Perhaps Madame de Staël was right, perhaps he had been a little in love with her and she with him; in any case, her kindness had helped make his stay in England bearable. For her the future was bleak. Before long she would have to leave Mickleham for Ireland. Her beloved son Norbury would be separated from her; in the damp and discomfort of Ireland the consumption which had always been a danger to her would re-assert itself. She would die without ever seeing her sister again.

D'Arblay went with Narbonne to see him off. 'I don't suppose two sadder faces have ever been seen,' he told his wife. Fanny was pregnant and unwell. He had left her with Susanna; nothing less than his friendship with Narbonne, he declared, could have induced him to leave her at such a moment.

'I would have liked to have made the journey less disagreeable for my friend; but all the efforts I made to appear less absorbed in my own anxieties resulted in mere grimaces. My friend, for his part, was quite unaware of the sacrifices I was making for him. He seemed painfully occupied in going over all the misfortunes of the last five years; his departure seemed to have re-opened all the wounds which the loving care he'd received in this country had cicatrised.'

Narbonne left Dover on 20 June, travelling under the name of Smith for fear of the hostile reactions he might meet from governments and royalist émigrés on his way to Switzerland. The voyage was stormy. 'I set out tomorrow very thankful, I assure you, that the rest of the journey is on land,' he wrote to the Locks on arriving at the Hague, 'for except that I was not captured and dragged as a prisoner to Algiers or Paris, I suffered every other sort of misery during a crossing that lasted four days.'

But his reception in the Hague had been far better than he had hoped. Assuming his own name on arrival, he was greeted warmly by old acquaintances, even asked to dinner at the British embassy. Much encouraged, he decided to abandon his false name for the rest of the journey and to use his Spanish title, Lara.

The Terror in France was reaching its climax as Narbonne made his leisurely way across Europe. On 10 June the infamous law of 22 Prairial had been passed, refusing suspects the right of counsel and allowing only two verdicts – acquittal or death. In Paris the stench of blood in the Place de la Révolution had grown so great that the guillotine had had to be removed to the outskirts of the city. Robespierre reigned supreme, using terror to enforce his ideal of a virtuous republic.

On 27 July, or 9 Thermidor, deliverance came. Overthrown in the National Convention, Robespierre went to the guillotine, to which he had sent so many victims, that same day. The news of his execution sent a surge of rejoicing through Paris, through France and the rest of Europe. 'Every heart was filled with inexpressible joy,' wrote Madame de Staël. 'Such is the nature of human life that the cessation of suffering is the greatest happiness of all.'

Robespierre was dead, the worst of the Terror was over in France but the laws against émigrés, whether royalist or constitutionalist, remained as harsh as ever. It was still too dangerous for Narbonne or any of his friends to return to France. He arrived at last at Mézery, where Madame de Staël had taken a house, to find a group of fellow refugees, Mathieu de Montmorency among them, and Ribbing installed as her lover. Narbonne showed signs of displeasure, Madame de Staël affected to ignore them. Her thoughts were all for Ribbing. When Narbonne, stung by her indifference, sought to revive her feelings for him and spoke sharply of her new lover, she answered simply, 'I love Ribbing.' All the same her attachment to Narbonne as a friend was indestructible; with Talleyrand and Montmorency he remained in the charmed circle of her affections. 'I know no one,' she once wrote, 'who understands friendship and misfortune in as wide a sense as I do.'

Narbonne's jealousy, amounting to little more than pique, was not enough to make him leave Mézery or even to fall out seriously with Ribbing. One morning, after exchanging words the night before, he and Ribbing left the house at dawn. After several hours, when they had not returned, Madame de Staël became convinced that they must be fighting a duel over her. Her tears and hysterics at their absence were only ended when Narbonne and Ribbing returned home together in a high good humour late that evening, with a string of fish.

The affair with Narbonne was over. Not long after, with reproaches as passionate as those she had made to Narbonne, she broke with Ribbing to find a new attachment, as tempestuous but longer-lasting, with Benjamin Constant. But memories of her sufferings over Narbonne, perhaps the greatest of her many loves, continued to recur in her work. The fate of the exceptional woman, passionately in love but unable to damp her talents or her feelings to the mediocre style required by men, was a consistent theme, the remorse of the men, who having failed to understand her suffered agonies at her death, an equally consistent act of wishful thinking. Her own sufferings, fortunately, never led her to share the fate of her unhappy heroines. She continued to live and shine with extraordinary brilliance, diffusing life and intellectual movement round her, transmuting her deepening experiences into literature.

Fanny d'Arblay never saw Madame de Staël again though her husband remained in constant correspondence with Narbonne, who became the godfather of their son. Even in France, where she and d'Arblay went in 1802, at the time of the Peace of Amiens, Madame de Staël remained an embarrassing friend; her opposition to

Napoleon, who would shortly send her into exile, was already all too clear. On hearing of Fanny's arrival in Paris Madame de Staël immediately sent a cordial note, expressing her desire to see her again. Fanny's answer was carefully considered:

'Madame d'Arblay cannot but be flattered at Madame de Staël's great kindness. She will certainly have the honour of presenting herself at Madame de Staël's house as soon as possible.'

'It is not easy to have been more cold,' she wrote to her father, 'and the "cannot but be" is not a very flattering phrase.'

Fanny's prudence was perhaps excusable. D'Arblay's future in France depended on the First Consul's favour, and he had already incurred Napoleon's displeasure by refusing to serve in the French army if he had to fight against his adopted country, Britain. But it is pleasing to hear Narbonne, in the following year when Madame de Staël's banishment had been pronounced, declare his loyalty to her in a letter to Napoleon:

'With a warrant out against me, shortly before 2 September, I owed my escape and consequently my life to Madame de Staël. The more she has fallen into disgrace with the First Consul the less, I am sure, he could pardon me for denying my sentiments of gratitude and friendship.'

A final scene brings back the memory of Juniper Hall. It was 1815. The war with France was over. Susanna Phillips had died of consumption fifteen years before. Narbonne, who had served as Napoleon's aide de camp, had been killed at the siege of Torgau in Saxony. The d'Arblays were making their farewell visits in Paris before leaving France.

'M. de Talleyrand Périgord,' wrote Fanny, '*ci-devant* Evêque d'Autun . . . came into Madame de Laval's Drawing Room during my visit of leave taking. He was named upon entering; but there was no chance he could recollect me, as I had not seen him since the first month or two after my marriage when he accompanied M. de Narbonne and M. de Beaumetz on a Wedding congratulation to our cottage at Bookham. I could not forbear whispering to Madame de Laval, next to whom I was seated, How many *souvenirs* his sight awakened! . . . M. de Narbonne had gone who made so much of our social felicity during the period of our former acquaintance; & Mr

Lock was gone, who made our highest intellectual delight; and Madame de Staël, who gave it a zest of wit, deep thinking & light speaking, of almost unexampled entertainment.— & my beloved Sister Phillips, whose sweetness, intelligence, Grace & Sensibility won every heart. All these were gone, who all, during the sprightly period in which I was known to M. de Talleyrand, had always made our society . . . Ah! What parties were those! how delectable, how select, how refined though sportive, how investigatively sagacious, though invariably well bred!

'Madame de Laval sighed deeply, without answering me . . . I left M. de Talleyrand to Madame la Duchesse de Luynes, & a sister whose name I have forgotten, of M. le Duc de Luxembourg, & another lady or two . . . till I rose to depart: & then passing by the chair of M. de Talleyrand, who gravely & silently, but politely, rose & bowed, I said: "*M. de Talleyrand m'a oublié, mais on n'oublie pas M. de Talleyrand—*". I left the room with quickness, but saw a movement of surprize by no means unpleasant break over the habitual placidity, of the nearly imperturbable composure of his general – & certainly *made up countenance.*'

Today the setting of Juniper Hall has scarcely changed, its tall windows looking out across a view of woods and fields and grazing cows. Inside, as befits a study centre, the rooms are functional and simply decorated, though graceful mouldings here and there attest to former elegance. But one room transports one instantly into the past. The sculptured drawing room has been restored to all its earlier magnificence by the Field Studies Council, its exuberant plaster-work and classical medallions crisp and white as wedding-cake icing against the pastel colours of the walls and ceiling. Empty of furniture but not of ghosts, it is still possible to imagine it animated once again by the laughter and conversation of its eighteenth-century guests who, at a time when their world was crumbling around them, refused to abandon their high spirits, their intellectual curiosity or their loves.

Books consulted

Arblay, Madame d' (Fanny Burney), *Evelina*, Everyman, 1917
  Cecilia, World's Classics, Oxford University Press, 1988
  Camilla, World's Classics, Oxford University Press, 1983
  The Wanderer, London, 1814
  Memoirs of Dr Burney, London, 1832
  The Diary and Letters of Madame d'Arblay, edited by Charlotte Barrett, Macmillan, 1905
  The Journals and Letters of Fanny Burney, edited by Joyce Hemlow and others, Clarendon Press, 1972–1978
Balayé, Simone, *Madame de Staël*, Editions Klincksieck, 1979
Bernard, J. F., *Talleyrand*, Collins, 1973
Blennerhassett, Lady, *Madame de Staël et son temps*, Louis Westhauser, 1890
Burney, Sarah Harriet, *Clarentine*, London, 1796
Castelot, André, *Talleyrand ou le cynisme*, Librairie Académique Perrin, 1980
Cooper, Duff, *Talleyrand*, Jonathan Cape, 1964
Dard, Emile, *Un Confident de l'Empereur, le comte de Narbonne*, Librairie Plon, 1943
Diesbach, Ghislain de, *Histoire de l'émigration*, Librairie Académique Perrin, 1984.
  Madame de Staël, Librairie Académique Perrin, 1982
Ehrman, John, *The Younger Pitt*, Constable, 1983
Golovkine, Comte Fédor, *La Cour et la règne de Paul 1er* [description of Narbonne and Ribbing's fishing party], Librairie Plon, 1905
Hahn, E., *A Degree of Prudery*, Barker, 1951

Hemlow, Joyce, *The History of Fanny Burney*, Clarendon Press, 1958

Herrold, J. Christopher, *Mistress to an Age*, Hamish Hamilton, 1957

Hill, Constance, *Juniper Hall, a rendezvous of certain illustrious personages during the French Revolution, including Alexandre d'Arblay and Fanny Burney*, John Lane, 1904

Kelly, Linda, *Women of the French Revolution*, Hamish Hamilton, 1987

Kilpatrick, Sarah, *Fanny Burney*, David & Charles, 1980

Macaulay, Thomas Babington, *Critical and Historical Essays*, Dent, 1843

Orieux, Jean, *Talleyrand ou le sphinx incompris*, Flammarion, 1971

Scholes, Percy, *The Great Dr Burney*, Oxford University Press, 1948

Sermoneta, Duchess of, *The Locks of Norbury*, John Murray, 1940

Staël-Holstein, Baronne de, *Oeuvres complètes*, Treuttel et Wurtz, 1820–1821, in particular:

    De l'Influence des passions sur le bonheur des individus et des nations
    Considérations sur les principaux événements de la Révolution française
    Réflexions sur le procès de la Reine
    Corinne
    Delphine
    Correspondance générale de Madame de Staël, vols i and ii, edited by Beatrice W. Jasinkski, Jean Jacques Pauvert, 1963

Lettres à Narbonne, edited by Georges Solovieff, Gallimard, 1960

Villemain, A. F., *Souvenirs contemporains d'histoire et de la littérature*, Didier, 1854

Watson, J. Steven, *The reign of George III*, Clarendon Press, 1960

Weiner, Margery, *The French Exiles, 1789–1815*, John Murray, 1940

Periodicals

Revue d'histoire diplomatique, 'Lettres de M. de Talleyrand à Madame de Staël, tirées des archives de Broglie', 1890

Achille Biovès, *Nouvelle Revue*, 'Madame de Staël, Narbonne et leurs amis à Juniper Hall, 1792-1794'

Manuscripts

Burney papers in the Henry W. and Albert A. Berg Collection, New York Public Library

Letters of Mrs Phillips in the Barrett Collection of Burney papers amongst the Egerton manuscripts at the British Museum

Index